MEN IN MIDLIFE

THE FACTS...
THE FANTASIES...
THE FUTURE

JOHN CLAY

SIDGWICK & JACKSON

LONDON

First published in Great Britain in 1989 by
Sidgwick & Jackson Limited
1 Tavistock Chambers, Bloomsbury Way
London WC1A 2SG

ISBN 0 283 99617 X

Photoset in Great Britain by
Rowland Phototypesetting Limited
Bury St Edmunds, Suffolk
Printed and bound in Great Britain by
Mackays of Chatham PLC, Chatham, Kent

MEN AT MIDLIFE

THE FACTS...
THE FANTASIES...
THE FUTURE

Who are all those people you have brought with you?
The disciple whirled round to look.
Nobody there. Panic!
Lao said: 'Don't you understand?'

Chuang Tzu

Nel mezzo del cammin di nostra vita
Mi ritrovai per una selva oscura
Che la diritta via era smarrita.

Dante – *Divine Comedy*

(In the middle of the journey of our life
I found myself in a dark wood
For the straight path was lost.)

Contents

Preface

I first thought of writing this book while I was writing a biography of Ely Culbertson, the contract bridge supremo. In his early forties, he underwent a midlife crisis, forsaking the fame he had achieved in bridge to develop an international World Peace Federation. This was an attempt to bring together in political terms the two disparate halves of his make-up – he'd had a Russian mother and an American father. Culbertson examined the past successes of his life and found himself wanting. He wrote, 'My life has been a series of failures. I have failed as a scholar, as a revolutionary, as a saint, as a sophisticate, as a husband. Only in material things have I attained success.' I remember at that time also reading Elliott Jaques's paper, 'Death and the Midlife Crisis', and being struck by its emphasis on working through the midlife crisis to a renewed appreciation of life.

Shortly after completing the biography, fate took a hand in my own life. As I moved into my forties, two crucial sets of events happened – both my parents died and I became a father for the first time when my wife and I adopted three children at once, two sisters and a brother.

The death of my parents, both within the space of one year and both from cancer, brought sharply into focus my own perception of mortality. I knew that I was next in line, confronted now consciously for the first time by the prospect of my own eventual death. As my father lay dying in the intensive care unit of Basingstoke hospital, his life-support system switched off, I was present at the moment of death, actually holding his arm feeling a sort of transmission, a handing-on. My mother had died a year earlier in the same hospital and had lain comatose for the last few weeks with a brain tumour. It gave me plenty of time to reflect on her life and our relationship together. She was a talented painter and photographer but had underused these abilities throughout her life, not always through her own choice. She had made up for this to some extent in the last three or four years of her life, once she realized her days were numbered. As I watched her dying I took stock, in my midlife, of the importance of not wasting opportunities and of coming to terms with my own limited time available. I knew I ought to make use of my abilities, here and now.

The death of parents has profound psychological effects. I was on my own, no longer answerable to them nor living in their shadow. With three vibrant, attractive children to be a father to, our lives brought together by the welcome hand of fate, I knew I had responsibilities not to let them down, to give them a sense of future as part of the continuity of my own life. I started writing books and broadened my professional life by taking a special interest in midlife as an adult psychotherapist. New departures and changes of direction were precipitated by my own midlife experience.

This book is the outcome of these developments. I have set out to explore the issues of midlife and try to unravel some of their complexity. Robert Burton sitting down to write *The Anatomy of Melancholy* in 1621 stated, 'I write of melancholy by being busy to avoid melancholy' – every author purges his own soul in the course of his own writing.

Acknowledgements

I am considerably indebted to my colleague Sarah Weston for conducting most of the interviews for this book. Altogether more than sixty-five men were interviewed, the youngest being thirty-five and the oldest just over fifty. We tried to cover as wide a cross-section as possible. We include men who underwent a midlife crisis as well as those for whom midlife was essentially a transitional period in their lives that presented issues needing to be addressed.

To reflect personal experiences as much as possible, we preferred not to use questionnaires, but encouraged people to find their own idiom in expressing their experience of midlife. Most interviews were of one hour's duration, sometimes longer. We hope that it is the contributors' voices that come through in this book – midlife is both a common experience and unique in the way it manifests itself to each individual.

Names and background information have been changed to preserve anonymity. I am most grateful to all those who gave their time in the making of this book and who were prepared to disclose their experience of midlife with such openness and frankness, testimony perhaps to the increasing importance of this stage of life.

I should like to give a special word of thanks to Robert Smith and Gill Paul for their help in shaping the book, and to Anne Kemp for transcribing the interviews.

1

Men and Midlife

There is another man within me that's angry with me, rebukes,
commands and dastards me.

THOMAS BROWNE

As long as you are trying to be something other than what you
actually are, your mind merely wears itself out. But if you say
'This is what I am, it's a fact that I am going to investigate,
understand', then you can go beyond.

KRISHNAMURTI

Adulthood is surrounded by myths. A central one is that maturity is an inevitable part of the ageing process, the older you get the more mature you necessarily become. Hence the shock at midlife for many men between the ages of thirty-five and fifty when they discover otherwise. Their lives have been full of activity and purpose and now they suddenly feel adrift, cast up in a no man's land, uncertain of the future, even less sure of the past and its fragile achievements. The expected unfolding of maturity hasn't arrived, they may even find themselves captive to emotions they hoped to have left behind in adolescence or infancy. The discomfort becomes so great that many 'act out' to avoid it.

Denial, by pretending that nothing has changed or, at the other extreme, by intensifying activity, is often a first reaction. Others make a desperate bid to escape by defying time, having an affair with a younger woman or, even more extreme, pitching themselves into a final bid for self-enhancement through gambling, drink, drugs or sex. All this is papering over the cracks, trying to fill up the inner void where their emotions and feelings ought to be. For men, much of adult life is spent filling this inner hole with outside achievement and outside success, often at the expense of the inner self and the capacity to trust, love and be loved. Such a person has

I

lost touch with his experience of himself, and now this inner man demands to be noticed. He's saying, 'I want to be heard. It's my turn now.'

A midlife crisis is often the outcome. It catches people by surprise. Richard Castle, an advertising executive, remembers being at Oxford Circus tube station and suddenly losing his nerve, unable to face going to his office or meet his colleagues. Yet he was a successful and esteemed businessman who had given no prior indication of difficulty. He had suddenly come unstuck. Why? Beneath the surface his life had been a series of compromises which had been tolerated up to then but which now suddenly began to overwhelm him.

A 43-year-old father of two adolescent sons became agonized by the realization that 'My children no longer respect me. They pass me by and are suspicious of my motives. I feel unwanted, impotent.'

James Goren, a stage designer aged thirty-nine, with notable achievements at Stratford and Shaftesbury Avenue described his feelings: 'Success is a funny thing. You get carried along by it, moving from one job to the next, without pausing to think. I was riding high, floating on air, seemingly without a care in the world. Yet a nagging doubt started to crop up. People kept saying how pleased they were with my work but it had no effect. I still felt empty.'

Midlife calls for reassessment, for taking stock. What have I achieved? How real are my close relationships? How well do I know myself? Am I really as successful or as mature as others see me? Will I have to accept that I am never going to make my mark on the world or write that masterpiece? What am I going to do about this persistent child-in-the-man that obstinately refuses to go away and whose demands are increasing? Where will I find meaning in my life?

It is a time for self-examination. It calls for a shift in relationships at work as much as at home. As Jung put it, 'You cannot live in the afternoon of life according to the programme of life's morning.'

The evidence in this book points to the fact that nearly all men experience midlife as a turning point. Partly because midlife is under-recognized as an important stage compared to infancy and adolescence and partly because men in our culture are traditionally reluctant to air their misgivings and stress at this time of life, relatively little attention has been given to it. Many men seem to get by at midlife, mainly because their symptoms are undetected and are often absorbed within the family or close relationships.

The most pressing question is: Why do some people have a midlife crisis and others not? Some individuals are clearly crisis-bound, leading too much of a one-sided existence, so that any untoward event may tip the balance against them. Yet others in broadly similar circumstances do not get a midlife crisis. This book sets out to look at three dimensions of midlife – midlife as crisis, midlife as transition, midlife as continuation.

What are the signs of a midlife crisis and what does it look like? Advance warnings are not always clearly signalled. A man may seem to be coasting along serene in his understanding that all is well and looks set to continue that way. Suddenly something unexpected happens – loss of a job, bust-up of a marriage, a personal tragedy – and he is plunged into a crisis. The first indications that a crisis is taking place may be a giving-up in certain areas, a gradual severing of the links with the past, loosening of the bonds of the present way of life. These are part of an early warning system that major changes lie ahead. Internally the defences that have served adequately for a lifetime may begin to weaken, a 'hidden' side to the person's nature begins to appear, and to those around him he may indulge in uncharacteristic behaviour, marked by rejection of outside help and increased self-pity. He asks to be left alone. He is entering a period of self-estrangement.

Typically a person may flounder around at home, listlessly moving from one thing to another, flaunting the emptiness of his life, beset by an inability to enjoy anything. He may retreat into self-absorption or into melancholy. His mood will swing between arrogance and self-abasement ('I'm no good, I'm useless'). Every aspect of his life comes under question. Horrified by much of what is revealed, he may become full of self-recrimination.

Or, more dramatically, he will act out his distress and go off the rails completely. He may make compulsive attempts to remain young, show excessive concern over health and appearance, indulge in increased sexual activity to prove youth and potency.

Either way he has lost direction, he's in Dante's dark wood, unsure of the way ahead. Depression may follow, seemingly unheralded, a puzzle to its owner. He may not 'see' what's going on, and blame his depression on outside factors, money, his job, politics or whatever. Depression, being to do with loss, is here the loss of the familiar, even well-loved, former self and all that the person has put together as his adult self. The agonies of self-appraisal, of self-doubt that accompany this depression are a necessary stage to go through. It is a process of shedding the old before taking on the new, or rather a way of unscrambling the package before putting it together again, letting go instead of clinging on to the past. Depression in this way can be a beneficial experience, a working through of the changes required by midlife.

This period of living with uncertainties is the turning point of a midlife crisis. Some people get stuck at this stage, unable to surrender the 'former self' clinging tenaciously to old habits and attitudes. Here the 'unfinished business' of childhood plays its part, reviving memories of abrupt changes in earlier relationships, of unmet dependency needs, of anxiety-provoking separations in early childhood and infancy. At midlife a man may fear to go through that again, and even to his detriment may prefer to remain in his present distressed state rather than risk changes that might reawaken earlier traumas.

Alan Whitehead discovered his wife was having an affair with a much younger man, recruited by him to give his children extra tuition. Shocked, he set about trying to reimpose strict controls on his relationship with her, get it back to where it was before, rather than talk to her about her own needs that were expressed in the extra-marital relationship. As an infant, he had been separated from his mother for some years and the thought of another separation at this stage of life overwhelmed him and blocked out his judgement of the situation. He panicked into re-imposing stricter control in a desperate bid to return to the *status quo*, and ended up with the opposite of what was intended, that is, more distance between himself and his wife and greater likelihood of their separation.

Few men can get through a midlife crisis unaided. To move on, help is needed. The role of helper (wife, partner, friend, therapist or whoever), is often crucial, to hold and support the person through this crisis. This may mean balancing the changes for him, mirroring what is happening and pointing out underlying factors, or perhaps just acting as an unequivocal, massive support.

The final stage of a midlife crisis is re-integration and self-renewal, an acceptance of what has happened as being necessary. It's putting the package back together again, and in so doing completing an important developmental task, the full-scale self-examination that midlife seems to call for. Having lived in uncertainties, listened to inner voices, to 'other voices in other rooms', to the promptings of the hidden side of his nature, a midlife man is now in a position to have a clearer assessment of himself, his abilities, his priorities, his strengths and weaknesses and the value of his relationships. He has 'seen the future and it works'. Rather than regret the loss of youth and of opportunities missed he can safely mourn their passing and move on to an appreciation of what he does in fact have. Nor need he be afraid of change, nor ultimately of death. Once he has accepted the inevitability of death, he can start living. Such an acceptance gives a sense of purpose to the rest of his life. He can feel comfortable with his 'one and only life cycle as something that had to be and that, by necessity, permitted of no substitution'. It really is his life he is living, not that of his parents or grandparents or colleagues. He can look forward to the future with equanimity.

A midlife crisis, then, is a challenge – meet it right and you can come out on the other side with renewed vigour and insight.

But men do not like to appear vulnerable. They are brought up to go it alone, especially in relation to personal difficulties. Seeking help is felt to be unmanly. Midlife exacerbates this problem. How can a man accustomed all his lifetime to hiding his emotions now suddenly admit to feelings of weakness and dismay? His upbringing has been to generate a self-image of competence and self-reliance. As a growing boy he was praised for his toughness and bravura and any overt display of emotion would be termed sissy, effeminate, a sign of weakness. His motto has become 'I can manage.

I can cope.' Very little in his adult life prompts him to change this. Substitutes for the first intimacy with mother are readily found – power, money, sex. Marriage can be a means of perpetuating this, the wife becoming a replacement or echo of the lost relationship with mother. The husband may manoeuvre himself into the position of a sort of 'superchild' looked after by the equivalent of a mother/mistress.

A further difficulty for many midlife men has to do with their underlying assumptions about their place in society. In the past, midlife men, especially those brought up on middle class values, felt secure in the belief that they would be sustained for most of their careers by that system; they felt confident that even if they didn't succeed individually, they had something to fall back on: the fail-safe of the system, of society's dominant values. Now men find themselves pushed back on their own resources, they cannot be guaranteed a clear run from cradle to grave buoyed up by the reassuring structure of a patriarchal society with its collegiate atmosphere. Nor does man's position as sole breadwinner and head of family remain in place any longer, giving him needed confirmation of his importance within the family. More and more a picture emerges of a weak and passive father, undermined, unsure of his identity.

To compensate for this lack of support in the public domain, men look to various forms of self-cure, as if the care of the inner man can only be undertaken by themselves. Looking after their own bodies and the twentieth-century urge to lead an examined life are two prime examples. It ' is as if the care of the inner man can no longer be entrusted to the state, to the public realm. Hence the recent growth in preoccupation with the politics of the body – as evidenced by fitness and health foods – attempts to give a meaning and solidity to life that cannot be found elsewhere. Look at the phenomenal success of the Body Shop and the number of recent films, on body-swap for instance, that mirror this.

Preoccupation with health and fitness has bred the so-called narcissistic type who takes refuge in himself and in his own self-absorption. Such a person exhibits a serene self-sufficiency and seeks to live in a world where dependency on others is reduced to a minimum. A cult of relationships replaces long-term commitment, liaisons are short-lived. Appearances become deceptive as these types are often among the most successful members of society and carry off its glittering prizes. But deep down, beneath the apparent omnipotence, there is an inner emptiness that may surface at midlife. Their success has been purchased at a price, cut off from warm, easy interchange. Weaknesses which have been split off and feelings of helplessness and rage, dating back to infancy and suppressed during adulthood, begin to re-emerge. In desperation they will seek to triumph over this by denying their need for emotional dependency on others; yet the more they try to deny this, the greater their emotional hunger becomes. It explains why such seemingly successful individuals often say they can find no meaning to their lives, that their success seems hollow. For some, unable to hold back the tension, a collapse or breakdown may follow.

The impact of the women's movement has certainly contributed to men's unease. Having dented previous self-assurance it has led men to be much more self-critical. But it has yet to reap the full benefits of shared responsibilities at home and equality at work. The so-called New Man has yet to emerge or if he has is often rather a suspect person suffering as much from role confusion as role improvement. Is he really seeking to share domestic tasks on equal terms or is he covertly engaged in a delayed exercise of getting back to the long-lost folds of mother, and seeking to please her, now embodied as Woman? For men the reality of separation from mother is a hard task, and an alarming one; they may never feel completely free, yet remain beholden to a person they are never going to become. Oscar Wilde put this succinctly: 'All women become like their mothers. That is their tragedy. No man does. That's his.'

In the workplace, men previously counted on the protective embrace of large-scale organizations to see them through their working life. Now with changing work patterns and the impact of a youth-orientated culture, midlife is at times felt to be the end of the line. Old age lies ahead, unwelcome, no longer the repository of wisdom, nor dignified by respect from the young. Ironically the highest compliment you can pay someone nowadays is the quip, 'You don't look your age.'

So who is this present-day midlife man, child of essentially traditionalist child-rearing patterns, with or without Dr Spock, and product of the sixties 'revolutions' in lifestyle? Is he more enlightened, more able to deal with the complexities of modern life? There's a Zen saying 'After enlightenment, the laundry.'

It's tough going to be a midlife man now, but as we begin to see in the next chapter, midlife can have its rewards. Even a full-scale midlife crisis, far from being something to be dreaded, can be positive and valuable. In keeping with the Chinese ideogram, crisis can equal opportunity.

2

Changeover

I have a simple philosophy and that is that every time you fail, it's really the real key to success because all you do is dust yourself off, and jump up on your feet and get going again because you've learnt a valuable lesson. So the more you fail, the more likely you are to succeed. Most people spend their lives failing once and then retreating from the failure and saying 'Well, I've failed it, I ought to do something which is less demanding.' I've always thought of failure as the most wonderful opportunity to succeed. If you go bankrupt, then you know you oughtn't to make those mistakes again, so next time you're going to be much better.

Bruce Cantlie was all set in the midst of a very successful career in advertising and as owner of his own advertising agency. He had a large swimming pool, a mansion and a big garden. His children were just finishing private school and ready for Oxford. Then, one night, aged forty-five, he found himself working on a new business schedule and, as was his habit, he stayed up most of the night doing this.

I got up from my study to look out into the garden and as I turned round I caught sight of myself in the mirror and saw this 5-ft 7-in little man with red eyes, a full night's growth, a large beer gut hanging over his belly and a back that was aching and sore. I suddenly realized that I would be dead in five years if I went on like this. I looked across to the desk and there were five empty packets of Dunhill cigarettes, I'd opened a new carton that same night, and in the bin under my desk were seventeen empty cans of beer and I thought 'This is absolute nonsense.' I went and had a shower, shaved and next day went in and resigned my job. Ever since that day I haven't had a drink or smoke.

I put myself in hospital for three months and had an operation I'd been putting off for several years for multiple spinal fusion. It meant lying still for three months in plaster of Paris from my neck to my ankles without moving a limb. Every two hours two male nurses would come in and turn me onto my stomach and two hours later back onto my back. After two days I suddenly realized that the ceiling of my hospital room was virtually an A4 page so I started to type on the ceiling in my mind. At the end of the three months when they tore away this plaster, I had written synopses for seventeen books on the ceiling and I had also worked out a sort of game plan to take me through the next ten years.

Now, it wasn't all that difficult because I was a reasonably wealthy man at that stage. I left hospital and the doctor said to me that I would always walk with a walking stick because of my spinal problems and I looked at him and, to be perfectly frank, I said to him 'You're out of your fucking mind – there is absolutely no way.' I started to swim the day I came out of hospital and I swam for an entire year until I could do a mile a day in a swimming pool. Finally like some weird salamander I crept out. Then I started to run, and took that up. Two years after I'd had the spinal fusion I ran my first marathon at the age of forty-seven and I've run in them ever since then because a marathon is sort of my yearly test.

That proved to me that I had all the stamina I needed. So I sold my agency to some huge multi-national for an indecent amount of money. I decided that I still had three years or so before I needed to change my life entirely. In fact I had told my wife at the age of twenty-five, that I was going to have two lives: the first life would be for her and the kids and for all the usual nonsense like cars and houses and education and holidays and things like that. The second life was going to be entirely for me so I would really do my job as a husband until I reached the age of fifty-five and then I wanted all the rest of my life to myself. At the age of twenty-five, it seemed like a long time away. Anyway here I was forty-five and sort of feeling that I'd done it all badly although I suppose by any standards I was wealthy and successful.

I wanted to keep to that plan. I now had enough money for my wife to live in the manner to which she had absolutely no right to become accustomed, and I could get on with the second life. I was going to become a writer but I figured that everyone has to learn their craft and whilst I had been a copywriter most of my life I still wasn't presumptuous enough to think that I could just write books straight off, so I thought 'I'll write three practice books' and I gave myself three years to do that, one book a year exactly. My wife said to me 'Look, I don't want you around whilst you're writing three practice books because you will be totally intolerable. Why don't you take a job and write your practice books in your spare time?' So I thought I would try that. I got a job with another advertising agency as their creative director. This was an enormous job and they offered me a huge amount of money – an absurd amount of money to do this job, so I thought 'Well I'll try working a ninety-hour week'. I'd worked sixty hours all my life anyway. With a ninety-hour week, I'd give them forty-five and I'd keep forty-five for myself as a writer. I'd write a short novel in the first year and then I'd write two more. Then I'd actually go into this persona as a writer, having three practice books under my belt and the fourth one was *bound* to be published because I'm a hugely confident human being and I'd done my homework, and if you've done your homework you ought to be rewarded.

So I worked this ninety-hour a week which involved getting up at 3.45 every morning and going to bed at midnight, and having half-an-hour for dinner at night. I took an hour off at lunch time to run and I ran ten kilometres every day and I kept this up, including two eighteen hour shifts on a Saturday and Sunday, for an entire year without missing a day. It got to midnight on 8th June 1987 which was the end of the first year and I hadn't finished the book, which was now eleven inches high and weighed 6½ lbs in manuscript and I started to cry and my wife had never seen me cry under any circumstances and she came in and she said – it was on the stroke of midnight and the hall clock was going bong, bong, bong – and I just couldn't bear the idea that I'd taken a year and hadn't finished this book. She said 'Why on earth are you crying?' and I said 'I haven't finished this fucking book' so she said 'But you only started at 2.15 in the morning.' It was true! – I remember the exact time, I had been sitting up reading, because I'm somebody who only sleeps four or five hours a night anyway, and I tend to read until about two o'clock in the morning. I had been reading a particularly famous English novelist who writes beautifully and I suddenly realized that it was about the eighth book of a certain type that I'd read and they were all beautifully written, the English was superb and they were going absolutely nowhere and they were disappearing up their own rear orifices and I thought 'I am absolutely sick and tired of this kind of nonsense writing that is supposed to be literature' and I hurled it against the bedroom wall and woke my wife up – that's how she knew it was 2.15 – and walked through into my study and wrote four words and that was the day I started my book. So suddenly it was midnight a year later, and I had given myself a year to finish this first practice book and I hadn't finished it, so I wrote furiously and I finished at 2.17, so it took a year and two minutes to write this first book.

I just simply didn't know what to do with it, but I thought 'Well, it doesn't matter, it's a practice book anyway, I'll start the next one' which I did. Then I was running with a friend a few days later and I said 'What do you do with a book?' and he said 'Well, you find yourself an agent,' so I said 'Who's the best agent?' and he named somebody and said 'But she has a small business and only handles huge celebrities etc.' But being an ad. man I knew somebody who knew somebody who knew somebody and went through the back and she agreed that she would read the first chapter. I sent over this pantechnicon full of paper and six weeks later she phoned up and said 'Bruce, I really do believe you've written a remarkable book' and from that moment on, it sort of became a fairy tale book. It was sold for the most amount of money that a first book has been sold for in America. It's already made nearly a million and a quarter dollars in advances. It's been published into nine languages now and there are three more in the offing. After a week in Britain, it's number nine on the bestseller list, it's number two on the bestseller list in Australia and it's about to be launched in America. That's really the story – I mean, it's just fairy-stale stuff.

I'm well into the second one, it's a sequel. It's at least half done and it's turning out to be an enormous book. I'm going to Africa tomorrow, in fact, to do the research on it. As I say, it's the fairy tale come true but it means that if I can do it, or if some skilled guy who had never written a book before in his life can, at the age of fifty-three, sit down and write what looks like a world best-seller, then anybody can do it. That's lovely because it means that in this hard, cold, cynical world that there are fairy stories and that anything is still possible and that legend of coming up from nowhere and getting there, is still happening in this day and age.

He attributes his personal success to an attitude to life that has evolved over the years.

I have a simple philosophy and that is that every time you fail, it's really the real key to success because all you do is dust yourself off, and jump up on your feet and get going again because you've learnt a valuable lesson. So the more you fail, the more likely you are to succeed. Most people spend their lives failing once and then retreating from the failure and saying 'Well, I've failed it, I ought to do something which is less demanding.' I've always thought of failure as the most wonderful opportunity to succeed. If you go bankrupt, then you know you oughtn't to make those mistakes again, so next time you're going to be much better. I really see life as a boxing match. You go into the ring every day. Boxing requires three basic elements: great physical prowess; a tremendous amount of blood and guts; but most importantly it requires intellect. You bring all three together in the right combination, you win in the ring and you win in life.

He defines in practical terms his method for getting hold of success and staying with it.

I have this feeling that everybody in the whole wide world is climbing this immense cliff and we're all hanging on by our finger nails and everywhere you look there are bodies dropping off – dropping as they can't hang on any longer – and the guy who wins is never the guy who gets to the top. It's the guy who hangs on one second longer than anybody else and so I found in life that if you just hang in and hang on, you always succeed because everybody else drops off, and so success is always by default. It's never because you did everything, it's because you were there and everybody else wasn't.

He had what he calls 'a fairly rocky sort of a childhood'. He learnt 'to be street-smart fairly early on' though his school career was attended with success. 'I was one of those children who was bright, one of those dreadful people who you get at school who wins a scholarship and is captain of cricket and football and still gets double-first at university.' It was there he developed his 'particular neurosis to win', which has remained with him most of his life.

It is very simple, we all have a form of camouflage and very early in life we are told not to be ourselves. We take our children and we swaddle them in all sorts of conventions, of what is right and what is wrong, and before we really know what has happened, the child has become a respectable member of the family or a respectable member of society, and he or she gets totally buried. By the time they've finished being teenagers they are prototyped to the degree that they've entirely forgotten who they are. There is this hard chrysalis around them, which I call the camouflage, and there are two ways of camouflaging yourself in life: the first one is to become a non-entity . . . to be so average and so like everybody else that you disappear, that's a perfect form of camouflage. The second one is to be so far ahead of everybody else that nobody ever catches up with you, which is an equally perfect form of camouflage. I really believe I was the latter rather than the former.

We have a thing in Australia (where he lives most of the time) called 'the tall poppy syndrome'. It works like this. If you raise your head one inch above everybody else's it gets chopped down because we are the original egalitarian society, so you learn that the whole process is to keep getting chopped down because they can never pull you out by the roots and every season you grow a little stronger until in the end you are a real tall poppy and they can chop and chop and chop and chop and nothing happens and you've got this enormous stem and you're standing there in the sunshine and you're saying 'Look at this . . .' Only now, in mid-fifties, am I beginning to see what is underneath my camouflage. I can really sit down and say 'This is me' and this book that I have written is to a very large degree that statement.

Success, in his opinion, is always driven by fear or inhibition. In his case he defined it as the fear of 'being nobody'. He thinks back to his own childhood, where he came from a very poor family, but was lucky enough to be a gifted child. 'But the fear of being nothing, being poor, of not being loved, and all sorts of wrong fears stayed with me. Those fears remain and get buried and you end up showing only the parts of you that you like and that you think are going to work.' But he recognizes that the other parts, though less visible, are just as important. Success, he feels isn't always all that it's cracked up to be.

People look at successful men and women and say 'Wouldn't it be wonderful to be like them?' But look closely at what's driving them. Sometimes those people who appear to be comparative failures are the really successful ones in life. My grandfather was a huge failure in life, but an acutely successful man. He grew roses and read books and would entertain me for hours just by talking to me. He had a lovely clean, clear, beautiful mind, and he never worried about anything in his life and died an extremely happy man but today he would be considered to be an absolute failure.

Mention of his grandfather makes him think ahead to his later years.

I have an enormous energy – an energy that never stops and I certainly want to write to books, write lots of them. Then I'd like a third life for the last fifteen years of my life – that's sort of between eighty and ninety-five. I think that then I might even be wise, and I'd want to use that wisdom in a very peculiar way. I really believe that kids are having an awful time growing up and that it's getting tougher and tougher to be a teenager in particular, really hard work. It's an enormous burden. I think between eighty and ninety-five, kids will believe me because I'll be so old that I won't be an oldie or a parent or even a grandparent, and I intend to become a sort of kids' guru so that kids can talk to me and I can tell them that it really isn't all that hard, it's the way you go about it if you want to succeed. I think I might have something to say then that's worthwhile. Kids understand how extraordinarily funny life is and many old people do too and they can really be outrageous and unless you're outrageous with children, you can't communicate with them. Children love outrage, they love the absurdity and the impossible. Between eighty and ninety-five everybody will forgive me everything and I intend to be entirely outrageous. There could be some lessons in that because being outrageous is terribly important. Conformity is a disaster and it's destroying the world, absolutely destroying mankind. There is no progress in conformity, conformity is always past tense, it never ever reaches out and touches anything new and I'd like to get that idea across.

He has three children of his own, three boys with whom he gets on very well, and he recalls the time he used to spend with them when he was 'being the world's most stupid executive, pre-menopausal time, weighing 13½ stone, a beery, hard-drinking, hard-smoking executive.' But he did at least then have the foresight, in terms of consolidating his relationship with his children, of making sure he spent two hours with them every morning, usually between five and seven in the morning. He'd get them up, being an early riser himself, and spend these two hours with them, they'd make breakfast and discuss their homework, or if the weather was fine, they'd go sailing and fishing – all in the early morning. For him this meant they grew up with a father who always had time with them.

It worked terribly well. They never saw me at night because I'd never get home before nine or ten and sometimes midnight, night after night. I was always tied up in my business, a huge success maybe but going absolutely nowhere at 100 miles an hour. But they always knew me as a father who had time for them and curiously enough my 27-year-old son called me the other day and said 'Dad, I have a problem and I need to come and see you.' So I said, 'Yes, sure, come home.' I'm always up at just after four in the morning anyway, and there was a knock at the front door and I thought 'How curious, nobody knocks at this time' and this was my son. Instinctively, he'd come at five in the morning because he had a problem and he needed to talk about it and just all his life he'd realized that that was when he'd talked to me. I have a lovely relationship with them all, I mean, I love them just so tremendously.

With his unquenchable enthusiasm for life, had he any thoughts about what might happen afterwards?

That's a very difficult question. I have lived this life as hard as I possibly can, just in case nothing does follow, and I really think by the time I'm through with it, I'll be happy to call it quits. It's awfully silly to say I'm a non-believer, because I don't believe that. I just simply believe that you are given an opportunity and if you can see it, you ought to take it, and then if there is anything afterwards, you ought to be awfully humble if you get a nice part.

I've trained all my kids that failure was absolutely essential, because how else could they know? There is a very simple credo in life and it goes like this: 'After you've walked the well-known way, dare your genius to walk the wildest unknown path.' There's no point in walking down the centre of the yellow line. It's pointless. They've paved it, there are cars zooming past – thousands of people going in the same direction – you have to take the wildest unknown path. You may fail but think of all the new territory you have struck and then some days you reach the heights. You just suddenly discover new countries, new parts, new beings, new yous, and that's a wonderful thing about life. Really, I believe implicitly that within each of us there is a miracle, and I'm using these words quite deliberately, that we are forced to be in a channel because of this camouflage, because of this conformity. We are channelled into doing things: to arrange kids, to put meals into mouths, to pay for mortgages. Then, eventually, when we get to the point when all of that is over, we're so tired – or we believe ourselves to be so tired – and we are conned into the idea that this is what society really required of us.

Saul Bellow develops this idea in his recent novel *A Theft*: 'People have to be done with disorder, finally, and by the time they're done, they're also finished. When they back off to take a new leap, they realize they've torn too many ligaments.' Bruce only accepts part of that, and feels that within each of us 'there is a whole persona that is entirely different' waiting to emerge.

People should just tear away this camouflage and be who they want to be. Life really does begin after you've paid your dues – after you've said, 'Right, I've done all that – now it's my turn and my turn starts at menopause.' Menopause is the most wonderful illumination. What we really ought to do is just be intrepid and say to ourselves 'What have we got to lose?' You've paid for the house, the kids are out of your way, so you might as well go for it – write a book or a poem, dig a hole or plant a rose, or do something that you want to do. Every human being that you've ever met, when you start to talk to them and ask 'Now really, really, if you'd had your life over again, what would you have done?' People say, 'You know what I'd like to have been, I'd like to have been an air hostess on Aeroflot.' I mean, there's always something that somebody wanted to have been and that's the thing you ought to be. Or 'I'd really like to run a small restaurant at the base of the Himalayas.' Go and do it because in actual fact you've nothing to lose. What's happening if you don't do it is that you are starting to slide down the other side of the hill and die, and that's why people die, they die of boredom, they die for lack of interest.

There's one other clue that's very important and that is, you have to get fit again after the menopausal time. You have to look at your body and say 'I've abused it, I've messed it around, now I'm going to fix it up.' It takes five years. Five years to make it very strong and as young as a twenty-year-old's and then you've got the rest of your life with a strong clean body. You really have to give up – not give up, but be very moderate with – things like cigarettes and alcohol because they get in the way, they make you tired and you have to have all the energy in the whole world. You give them up not because they're bad habits but because they get in the way in a physical sense. You're going to need energy to be successful, there's absolutely nothing to stop anybody being successful after fifty because that's the time to be successful. After all, you've learnt the lessons, you've gained the wisdom, you can see what it's all about, looked around corners and you've got all the equipment to be successful – all you need is the energy. So fix up your body – that's very easily done. Any good sports medicine doctor will teach you how to take a body in bad repair and fix up so that it works extremely well. You don't have to run marathons or stupid things like that, you can just simply get fit again.

I have to end up with this lovely story. Like every ad. man in Australia, I own a Porsche; it's ten years old this year and I love it very dearly. I was at the red lights the other day when these two absolutely delightful teenagers were standing by and one turned to the other and said, 'Look at that man in the Porsche – what a dreadful waste.' I thought this highly amusing but then the other one turned round and said, 'They're all the same, these men in their menoporsche!'

3

At Work

Last night a storm
Blew down my roof.
Now I can see
The moon more clearly.

Japanese Haiku

A crisis is all pervasive. It takes somebody over. In the stories that follow, we see how the focal point for the crisis is likely to be located in one of the three major areas of a person's life – at work, in marriage, or in the sense of identity. Inevitably all three areas tend to overlap, but a crisis usually has a precipitating factor in one particular area. We start with two crisis stories that centre on work.

Thomas Westfield is a tallish, open, friendly man of forty-eight. He describes himself as 'a very imbalanced personality. Great strengths and appalling weaknesses,' a surprising description for someone who has made such a recent success of his life. His crisis happened after he had been working in New York for the American subsidiary of a large British company. He was suddenly fired at the age of forty-two, after a business plan he had tried to introduce onto the American market failed. The suddenness of these events took him by surprise. 'I don't want to make it sound too dramatic but it was a hell of a shock. It was a classic midlife crisis.' His wife was in England and altogether he had six children to support (from his two marriages), nor, at that time, did he have the consolation of capital to fall back on, such as a house. He took the first plane back to London and spent the next two months wondering what to do. As a first taste of unemployment, he paid an unaccustomed visit to the dole office.

It was actually such a private thing. It was absolutely grotesque. To find myself in a dole office at the age of forty-two with a lot of other people was absolutely the most shattering thing. I rushed out, not waiting for my turn. Sitting in my car I knew I had hit rock bottom. I suddenly realised 'My God, this is it.' But that was a sort of catalyst for turning everything around. The humiliation of that was something which shook me into a white heat of determination, to actually build a business and make it work.

I was always very bad in corporate life which is why I was fired. I am what I am – rather individualistic. In corporate life, with their tidying-up committees, always being subject to other people's decisions, I was very very bad at it. I made a lot of enemies, I think, through impatience and through frustration, not being able to lead the entrepreneurial life which is me. Terribly good thing I was fired.

He feels he detected in himself these entrepreneurial characteristics some time ago:

It sounds rather cynical how I am going to describe them. I think one characteristic is a contempt for money. I think if you become obsessed by safety you'd never do a thing. I mean, if you think about the 'down' side of things too much, if you are inevitably cautious in life, you simply can't get yourself to do the entrepreneurial thing. I think natural entrepreneurs just have to be entrepreneurs – you have to take risks, walking along the edge of a precipice, you get your kicks out of the fact that you *are* walking along the edge of a precipice and yet you are in control. I think all that was always inside me.

He brought back with him from New York 'a tiny seed of an idea in my mind which was a lifeline to hang on to.' In New York, he had been favourably impressed with the bookshops there, how they stayed open late and over weekends and encouraged visitors to browse unhurriedly, with knowledgeable staff and classical music often playing. A book-lover himself, it struck him that comparable places in London with a well-designed layout would be likely to succeed. He stitched together a financial package with the help of family, friends and the Government-sponsored BES scheme, so that six months after his crisis, his first shop was opened in September 1982. The 'white heat of determination' was paying off.

I wanted to set up bookshops like the ones in New York, full of books and chatty staff, friendly, unthreatening, slightly informal, literate but not elitist. There were enough people like me out there to make it work. At first we designed a simple store plan, an art student sketched it out for £25 and I filled the shops with the type of books which appealed to book lovers, not best-seller buyers. I aimed the whole thing at me really. I never doubted it would work although we had some pretty terrifying times to start with. Another entrepreneurial characteristic is to develop a complete confidence in what you're doing – a totally undeserved self-confidence which you develop and gain through business activity. Starting up your own business lets you use all your own strengths without actually planning to show your weaknesses. You needn't go into areas which are going to expose your weaknesses. I'm bad in committees, I'm bad subject to other people's whims, I'm impatient of other people's lack of drive, but here I can use all my strengths and make sure that other people pick up those areas which I'm bad at. Great privilege, much easier.

There's a strong identification now with the work he's doing.

This is me totally. Successful retailers aim their shops at themselves, they're an extension of their own personality. These shops do reflect the way I like to buy books personally – it's become the easiest piece of market research of all. They're like your children. I do buy a hell of a lot of books from them.

His company expanded steadily and now runs a chain of very profitable and highly acclaimed bookshops throughout the UK. More are planned. He looks back on this with justifiable pride.

The thing I love is the fact we started with 6 of us, and now 7 years later we have 580 employees and it will be over 600 by the end of this year. It's probably something like over 1,000 people I guess, actually being fed by this company. I love that. I know that's rather paternalistic but it gives enormous pride. Being responsible for these people is terrific.

Having got over his crisis, he sees it as producing a widening future. 'I'm forty-eight and feeling very well. I know the things we're going to try and do over the next ten years which are just so exciting, I can hardly wait to do them. I want to build this and have enormous fun building it and turn it into a really large company over the next decade.' Work is central to his present-day life.

If I'm away from business, I usually get very fretful – like on holiday. Perhaps it's this fear of the unknown thing. Sitting on a beach is just purgatory for me. If I'm not in action, I absolutely can't bear it. No, I can't stick inaction. I always feel completely relaxed really when I'm working because I can see what is going on and I know what the problems are, to be faced up to. What kills me on holiday is not knowing and having to do any amount of ringing up. I realise then there is probably more stress running through me than I thought.

He has his own repertoire of 'tricks' which he employs to avoid stress.

I'm never late to anything, not because of any other reason, but being late just fusses me to a degree which is quite unrealistic so I'm early for everything. I stop working at 8 o'clock or 8.15 in the evening and I then do something totally different and I won't work after that time. I play with the children – anything but work late at night because if I got tired then I can't sleep and sleep is absolutely essential. I do have a capacity for being able to block out of my mind things which could become obsessively worrying. I have developed a private technique of blocking them off in my mind and re-awakening them when I need to get in there. It's something that *has* to be faced up to. I make myself face up to it as quickly as I can. It's the fear of the unknown which is stressful. I have a policy: if there is a problem, face up to it.

He has been through what he himself terms a classic midlife crisis and come out of it with flying colours. Perhaps at one level he needed to provoke this crisis to get from where he was – a frustrated businessman – to where he ought to be – an entrepreneur in charge of his own show. But creating the crisis was one thing, weathering it was another. Deep down he knew it was a matter of choice, of wanting to do so.

I heard a sermon recently. I was struck by the simplicity of the statement, and I did so agree with it. I looked back on my own experience and I thought, 'How true, how very true!' The person giving the sermon was saying that the greatest gift of life at the end of the day is to have the capacity to choose life, and not death, to choose light and not dark. You know, we all have this. You can actually choose to go the wrong way, or you can choose life. Looking back, it was an enormous crisis when I lost that job, it really was, with small children at school and everything else, but I did actually choose to survive. One can choose not to survive. I'm saying that, I hope, not with conceit but with humility. I'm quite proud of it.

David Armstrong went through a crisis in his early thirties, and crisis has remained a refrain in his life as he's now involved in crisis work with the police. As a psychologist, he is brought in to handle the after-effects of serious incidents – a shooting, a hijacking, a diplomatic incident or whatever. He carries round with him a 24-hour bleeper and gives the impression of always being on the alert, as if there is not a moment to waste. He is a taut, thin, wiry man, bursting with energy.

If you're talking about 'midlife crisis' mine was definitely at thirty-one, without a doubt. It wasn't just the divorce. Up to that time I collected about seven or eight companies that were reasonably successful and then they went 'bang' and I found my partner had been pinching stuff left, right and centre. He subsequently committed suicide. Then my wife walked out on me and took the child and the furniture with her – went away with my best friend. I turned round and ended up working in a bakery, working nights whilst I did another degree during the day – so that was crisis time for me.

Midlife crisis for me was literally going from Chairman of this, that and the other – I manufactured ladies' tights, which I can assure you the fairies do not produce overnight by waving a wand – to literally packing bread in a bakery, because I needed the extra money as I wanted to do a psychology degree. All my money had gone by then. When I first went to university, I was taking psychology – that was in the very early sixties, but I gave it up then, put off by poeple who said 'You'll never make any money on it. What's psychology? What use is it to you?' At that time, probably they were right. I switched to business studies. Business consultancy was then 'the rage'. Eventually I did make money out of it as I ended up as joint managing director of a fashion group. Then I started out on my own and ended up with two export companies, three shops, a manufacturing plant that I'd literally built myself. Everything was going fine. But then in the 1974, the wheels fell off, the understatement of the century, and us being small and private we were one of the first people out. We didn't go out for much, but we went out nonetheless. I couldn't carry on. I think I probably would have bashed my way through it for another couple of years, making the whole thing worse, no doubt, if it hadn't have been for my partner, and my ex-wife. I don't blame her – I was doing it out of pure drive. It was pure energy and drive that was getting me places.

For the next few years he went through a period he defines as 'bloody rough – really rough. I was studying astrology at the time and an old palmist said to me that "By the time you're forty-three you'll be doing exactly what you want." I was only thirty-three at the time – it seemed a long way off but she was right.'

After his degree he eventually came to his present work as a police psychologist through a friend of his girl friend. Her husband was an armed policeman, and had been involved in

. . . what could only be called not just a tragedy, but an absolute trauma. The whole thing went wrong and a couple of their guys got their heads blown off and that sort of thing, and nobody even knew of a psychologist that was working in that sort of field and the ones that were contacted did not want to know, thank you very much. And I just went into it and said, 'Look, I know bugger all about it, I've never worked in that sort of work before but I'll have a go.' They said, 'If you'll have a go, we'll send you the people.' They sent me the whole lot and I got pretty good results. Eventually I influenced them to use hypnosis to get rid of nightmares and that sort of thing, and it just went right on from there. The Police Federation got to know about me, started sending me round to other police forces and I loved it. I'll never forget the first time they sent a squad around to my office, they arrived about 1.25 one afternoon and left at about just before 11 o'clock at night.

He now realizes that there has got to be 'an element of drama' in his work to sustain his interest in it.

My work is now very very unusual. I'm a specialist in trauma and shock – murder and rape, hijack, firearm situations, that sort of thing – just loving it, absolutely loving it. I'm not in an industry that's going to fall down – some of these hijackers keep pinching people. I think I'll be Ok. I came in the field just at the right time. I only started crisis work in 1983 and it turned out it was just the right time. The police didn't know what to do with their guns. They never thought anything could go wrong and the whole bloody lot went wrong. Nobody ever thought that journalists and envoys and people like that would ever get pinched. They just sauntered through the world thinking 'We're British, nobody will touch us.'

He can see now that, however accidental his getting into this field might have been, he needed to be in an environment that was going to be fully testing.

Everybody says psychologists have got hang-ups and although everybody's got a certain number of problems or hang-ups in their life, I was the classic. I mean, my mother died in childbirth. I was brought up as a Roman Catholic with a very very severe, strict father, who's mellowed dramatically over the last two or three years. I hated my childhood – I absolutely hated it. I had a step-mother – she was very pleasant – if she'd have just stopped trying to be my mother and just been herself, we'd have got along fine, you know. She always sided with my father. It was literally two against one all the time. My father was quite violent in his own way. For a long time I went through life thinking that I was the one that was wrong all the time. I really did. I didn't think that I was right on any of my ideas. Lancashire, where I was born, doesn't help. It can be very narrow-minded, very bigoted and I needed London, I really did. I love London. I like the anonymity. You can either have a friends week-end or you can have a nothing week-end . . . whatever time I finish work, and sometimes it can be quite late . . . you can do something if you want to do it – you really can. If I wanted a superior meal at 4 o'clock in the morning, you can always go to a casino, or you can do something. In Lancashire, you get stopped on the street for being out at that time. People say, 'What the hell are you doing?' It's even the sort of town where you're talked about if the landing light's on at 1 o'clock in the morning – that sort of place.

I constantly fought with my parents and thought, 'You're not going to dominate me.' Any suggestion of domination I used to crush – just hit – flat, bang, head-on, and then I didn't speak to them or contact them. Just to give you an idea of what I mean. When I rang my father up and said, 'I've got my psychology degree,' he said, 'What's that?' I said 'It's the study of the mind.' He said 'Oh, we don't believe in any of that – anyway what are you going to do with it?' I said 'Well, I've got a sort of job with the Health Service.' He said 'Oh – what are you going to do with the old chest you left under your bed? Do you want it, or shall we throw it away?' Oh, thanks dad, you know. Not a kind word, or a nice word or anything, but that was just the end and I just said 'Fuck off' and didn't speak to them for three years.

Then more recently my cousin said, 'Look, you know, they are getting a bit old.' My parents didn't even know where I was and that suited me fine. I thought 'I'm just not going through that sort of hassle anymore', and then my cousin said 'Look, you'd better understand they're getting a bit old you know.' My father was seventy-six at the time and I thought 'Yeah, I suppose that's right' and I just changed my attitude. At that time I was feeling a lot more comfortable and confident and things were going a lot better for me anyway, so I started getting a bit more emotional with them and calling my mum 'love' and sending drippy Easter and Christmas cards and all that sort of stuff, and they came to London and they really were very sweet. As a matter of fact the only person who put a sugges-tively semi-nasty comment in was me and I sort of stopped myself as soon as I said it. I thought 'Oh, why did I say that, it was quite pointless.'

As I say this is more my time. I've gone through a twelve-month period when I was bloody terrified, thinking 'Shit, this is it for the rest of your life', sort of thing and thinking 'What happens if, what happens if, what happens if?' but how could you ever correct all the 'ifs' that could possibly come up. I'm now more prepared to wait and see what the 'ifs' are and cope with them as they come along.

When he says 'this is more my time', he means he's now more fully in tune with his present life, no longer fighting the battles of yesteryear. There's more acceptance in his life. He feels more grounded. His present girl friend reflects these changes. Before, girl friends had to be 'beautiful, pretty and sophisticated'. Now he looks for personal qualities and his current girl

friend is 'much warmer than anybody that I've ever met before – very caring, very warm' and it's brought out a more caring side in him.

I'm forty-four now – and last year, without a doubt, was the best year of my life. I mean, it was just fantastic, really fantastic. I'd had a lot of trouble with property in London, but I'd managed to get something that I could afford. My girl friend is just fantastic – she's wonderful – she's the only girl I'd think of spending the rest of my life with. And yet, conversely she had a lousy year, really terrible year. Her brother died in August and for her it was awful, but for me it was really good financially. I mean, I netted £54,000 so that was quite enough for me to live on, thank you very much. Nothing went wrong.

But most of my last year's decisions and probably a few of the year before that as well, were based on the fact of Aids. That affected my decisions dramatically. I mean, I had virtually thought I'd got out of jail free, because I was a classic. In the past I'd had about eight or nine girl friends – one was on the West Coast of America, she was an American Indian, and as soon as it all blew up, I just thought 'Oh, shit – that's me – definitely me.' I went down to one of the units and they looked at me and I said 'Shut up and just do it' and I was alright, and I just thought 'Well, it really is about time I started to think about settling down'. My parents were now eighty and thought it was wonderful 'Ooh, I am pleased you're settling down at last.'

But it is his work that gives him the strongest sense of who he is and where he is going.

I enjoy my work. I'm doing exactly what I want to do. My work is a natural expression of me – it's not something that I've got to don a cloak and become another person in order to do, I just do it. There's a lot of change in my work, a terrific amount of change. You can be dealing with rape one minute and then be out at the front of a 15-metre police powerboat going down the Thames at 40 knots the minute after, or be on a parachute jump or something like that, so there's a terrific amount of change in my work. My bleep is on twenty-four hours seven days a week, Christmas Day, the lot. I can be called out anytime. I really do think that if I'm going to stay number 1 in the field, which at the moment I'm classified by Scotland Yard as being, I'd better bloody be there when something happens.

Being on call seven days a week gives me that element of comfort. Because it hasn't gone off in the last hour, I know there's nothing dramatic going on. If, as I now talk to you, I were relying on my office phone, it would mean I'd have to give them your number, the person's number that I'm going to next and so on. The police work twenty-four hours; the military work twenty-four hours; the Home Office work twenty-four hours.

He's totally involved in his work, which he now closely identifies with, and he recognises that the 'need to be needed' is of special significance to him, granted his past.

This sounds terribly arrogant and I don't mean it to be – I very often am arrogant and with the police you've got to be, otherwise they try to walk over you. I don't wish to sound arrogant about the way that I'm handling crisis work. First of all, I do not create a problem where there isn't one and I don't presume a problem where there isn't one either and neither do I give my client more bloody problems than he first came with. I really believe I've got it right and believe I can actually promote psychology as being an effective science now. It's come a long way from the old adage of 'if you've got to see a psychologist, you must need your head testing and all the rubbish therein'. It's taken a while to get the credibility and now I think I've got it I want to keep it in the front line – very much in the front line, plus as I said at the beginning, I do need an element of drama in my work, otherwise I just leave it alone. I can't do it.

I used to have a free-floating inferiority complex, in that if I'd not got something to worry about, I would be worried about the fact that I'd nothing to worry about, because something was bound to go wrong, and I was often more concerned with the 'ifs' and the 'tomorrows' and the 'next years' than I was about enjoying here and now. That's why I missed the trees, that's why I missed the Thames and didn't sort of look at it, and missed flowers and all those nice things in life. And I'm not prepared to do that anymore. I can be very very decisive in my work 'you will do this now' and I'm quite good at making sure that I'm not pissed around.

I live all the time with people on the edge. It is most likely in the course of the next year or two I will be shot, but whether or not that will mean a serious injury or just a casual injury, remains to be seen. I do a lot of talking down and that kind of thing, talking people down . . . I do a lot of hostage negotiation and I am aware that I am known of to a number of foreign agencies. I have done a number of front-line negotiations where the people on the other sides have been armed. There's quite a risk of being shot. I don't look at that very dramatically to be quite honest with you. It is not all that easy to kill somebody and I can assure you that I've been very heavily trained in self-defence to know what to do in a car or in a plane or whatever. Of course I'm very often armed myself.

Crisis work brings him face to face with the inner dramas of his life, his own crises of childhood. Now he feels he's emerging from the shadow of his father and his father's disapproval.

I look at my work and I want a Nobel Peace Prize. I *do* want a Nobel Peace Prize and therefore in every bit of my work that I do, I try to do it slightly better each time I do it. If I face a similar situation, I use the previous experience as an experience, not necessarily trying to make the two fit, but trying to do it better each time. So that I will be slightly more known and slightly more recognised so that I've got a chance of a Nobel Peace Prize. I really want one. I think it's probably the most effective reward that anybody could be given ever.

Jung has a phrase that the way of wholeness is full of fateful detours and wrong turnings. David Armstrong's life seems to bear this out. He has used the frustration of his childhood to mobilize himself into discovering what his right work milieu is.

Looking back, it was the best possible thing that could have happened because without all those things having come together at once, I think probably I'd have tried to start another few companies up or something like that, in other words, just start all over again – and it wasn't the field I should have been in anyway. It's almost like I had to do that before I was allowed to do what I should be doing. Well, now this is my time and I'm using it as my time.

Both the above stories show how central work is to a man's identity. It defines not only how he is seen in the eyes of the world, but much of his own self-esteem. Lose a job through dismissal or redundancy and that self-esteem can go into a catastrophic decline.

Studs Terkel in his book *Working* gives an example of this. Dr John Coleman, President of Haverford College, took an unusual sabbatical during the early months of 1973. He worked at menial jobs. In one instance, he was fired as porter-dishwasher. 'I'd never been fired and I'd never been unemployed. For three days I walked the streets. Though I had a bank account, though my children's tuition was paid, though I had a salary and a job waiting for me back in Haverford, I was demoralised. I had an inkling of how professionals my age feel when they lose their job and their confidence begins to sink.' As Terkel comments: 'Perhaps it's this fear of no longer being needed in a world of needless things that most clearly spells out the unnaturalness, the surreality of much that is called work today.'

So far as work is concerned, midlife is double-edged. It may mark the point where a man has reached the peak of his profession or it may be a signal to him that he has no further to go. Positions ahead of him are fewer, younger people are coming up and also competing for them. The dreaded stagnation looms.

Ken Saunders, a computer manager at forty-eight, feels 'stuck' and his

self-confidence is wavering. He's been with the same firm since he left school.

I have less control of my destiny than in the old days. My disillusionment dates from my early forties after my last re-grading. Then we were privatised and had this re-organisation. Work became just an illusion of activity for me. I don't think I bring anything personal to it, other people could do it just as well. At forty-eight it isn't all that easy to move and get a job outside and at the kind of level of responsibility I've got. I've never really actively gone out and looked for a job outside, not recently anyway.

He had put his faith all along in viewing his working life as a steady progression upwards, aiming for promotion at the next level 'achievable through one's contribution and experience, skill and so on. Now as one gets up the hierarchy there are fewer and fewer jobs and it seems to me that the avenue forward is really more of a greasy pole, it's more like being the diplomat, the courtier, the bullshitter. It's not to do with what you've done, it's all the yes men.' The tinge of bitterness that creeps into his remarks comes from what he perceives as lack of reward for his persistence. He concludes: 'It makes me wonder about what's going to happen to me in the future and what control I've got over my destiny and does it matter anymore?'

Roger Watkins has worked in a Government laboratory for twenty-five years. There are days when he thinks 'God, I'm a failure at my job. But it goes, I don't think that again for two years.' As midlife approaches he's beginning to notice missing dimensions in his job.

It isn't very people-orientated. I mean I can beaver away for days and the only conversation I have is 'How's the weather?' I do my own thing, with my own kit. Perhaps I'll talk with the man who works for me, but it's not very 'peopley'. I don't have to worry about people or have to talk to people, that's done by my branch heads. So perhaps I'm trying to search for something that will get me more involved with people.

Again there is a conflict emerging at midlife between the value of persistence and the need to find a more human face to work, what he calls its 'people' dimension.

Harder by far to face is dismissal or redundancy. Douglas Cameron, an engineer, was suddenly sacked from his company at the age of forty-two.

I felt quite bitter about it at the time and yet the other side of me said 'Well did I ever expect to retire with the firm?' It's just when you try and work harder and suddenly you realise it's not enough. It cost me a lot in self-confidence. I find I think twice before I stick my neck out these days, it's too painful.

No amount of re-assurance can ease the hurt for him. He saw himself as a company man, with loyalty and application high on his list of priorities. 'I thought the harder I tried to work, things would improve but it didn't seem to work that way.' He knew he was more of a 'tortoise than a hare' and in a world of go-getters he was slipping behind. The feeling of not being wanted when he felt he had abided by the traditional values of deference and duty he found particularly acute.

Maybe I don't stand my ground as well as I should. I used to when I was about thirty but after a couple of comments from other people, I realised I was pretty annoying in the way I did it, so I adjusted. It was probably my downfall. If I'd kept on being fairly direct, not worried about the consequence and so on, I would probably have been a director.

Peter Greenacre is disabled, suffers from a speech impediment and a lame leg. Now aged forty, he was made redundant a year ago. It was a shock to him as he had been with his company for eleven years. Having survived three rounds of redundancies, he had grown a bit complacent. Despite the warning signs and urgings from his colleagues, he sat tight, hoping he would be spared.

In the back of my mind I knew it was coming along because the company had been doing very badly, but when they actually tell you you're going, it knocks your ego basically. After a time it becomes water under the bridge. Time just goes by and you don't notice how it clocks round.

Once redundant he found he had become too specialized to change jobs easily. He had no one to fall back upon, being single. His outside interests were few. He joined a local drama group to help him with his speech, and to learn to breathe correctly and to act. But deep down the loss of a job had hit him hard. He sought help from MSC programmes and went on a redundancy course, but basically he's a loner, upset by the failure of politicians to help the poor and the handicapped.

I tell friends I'm redundant, but I don't go on about it. I tell them if they know of any jobs going to let me know. I try and get on with it. I'm not going to be depressed, or go out and shoot myself or anything. I've found I can cope OK. You get sad, though. You come to a point where you wonder 'Am I ever going to find work again?' When you get interviews that say 'no', that knocks you down but you pick yourself up. You take it day by day, week by week. I'm much more confident than I was at 35 but I've left it too late, and the future looks like a blank crystal ball. I've no idea what's going to happen. Don't see a lot of point in thinking about it.

Alan Day, at thirty-eight, lost his job in computing recently, annoyed because he felt it was a secure trade 'particularly for people that are changing career half-way through their lives'. He was axed as part of the company's reorganization. It forced him to look at his need for 'security' within a large organization, and understand how this and his reluctance to take on a managerial role and his avowed problems with 'authority' derived from his own upbringing with a dominating and tyrannical father. He's always backed away from looking at this but with the support of his partner Tony, with whom he is now living, he is beginning to look at it more openly. His partner is involved in running a helpline for Aids sufferers and is urging him now to concentrate more on his own needs and not to rush into things.

After I was made redundant he insisted that we sat down and tried to look at our finances and attempted to convince me that I didn't really need to be earning as much as I had been – that we would manage somehow, while I try and collect my thoughts and decide what I want to do.

Others continue to find midlife an unexpected challenge in their working life. Peter Fuller is a surveyor aged forty-four. He's still in the 'achieving' phase.

I still get up in the morning and think 'Good, it's another day again to go and have a crack at', whereas I had expected it to be 'Oh God, roll on sixty when I can retire and chuck it all in.' I'm not finished yet. I think funnily enough I've got more ambitious as I've got older. I don't think very much about my age. If you worry about how old you are, the effect is to hasten your old age. It's the one inevitability, isn't it – short of death – and it's bound to occur so why waste your time worrying about it? You might as well get on and make the most of what you've got.

Brian Calvert, an Inspector of Schools, has recently, at the age of forty-two, made a double move of house and job that's taken him back to the area of the country where he grew up.

I think life has never been better. I wouldn't want to be younger. I wouldn't want to be thirty again. Life has been enriched by the process of ageing when you look at it in terms of more senior posts, better pay, more comfort, less concerns than you had when you were twenty-five, shuffling bills, that sort of thing. I am quite satisfied with my life really and the way it has turned out is better than I could have thought.

He is contented with his life. The only shadow on the horizon is the prospect of his wife or one of his children dying. 'That would be a major fear in my life.' For him and for Roger Watkins the awareness of death is only just beginning to make itself felt at midlife.

Colin Mackintosh, another contented man, has at thirty-nine a rounded attitude to life: a good marriage, children, parents whom he is still fond of, a job that is fulfilling and a latterly-developed passion for opera and music.

On the whole I'm very positive about things and see lots of challenges in the future. So I don't tend to think about coming out of one era and going into another. At the moment it's a progression. The moment you start letting mortgage and family responsibilities take over and feel 'You must do this in order for that to happen' is the moment you start to get dissatisfied. I've seen that happen in some of my colleagues at work and in some of my friends and I'm determined to keep a grip on that.

Some years back in the Army he met two or three characters about whom he felt 'Goodness, they're not successful, but they enjoy life.' He thinks of this whenever he feels the 'rat race' is getting the better of him.

Laurence Kelly is an example of someone who risked leaving the security of a steady job as a partner in a firm of Chartered Surveyors seven years ago when he was thirty-seven to go freelance, working from home. However great the risk (he had school fees to pay for children in private education) he felt impelled to take it on.

I was earning more money then than I do now but there were a lot of strings attached and I was unhappy at times. It was all live now and pay for it tomorrow. Lots of people said what a crazy thing to do. You're giving up a secure income to take on something which could be a total disaster. As it turned out it nearly was, but I think it actually made a better person of me. As a result I got my business and personal life sorted out.

Now in his mid forties he feels a pleasing ambivalence and welcomes the flexibility his way of life gives him. He can go out and play tennis at midday or work until eleven at night. 'It both excites and irritates me.'

4

Identity Issues

Uneasy lies the head that wears a crown.

SHAKESPEARE

For the next two stories, work and the sense of inner identity are closely associated. Here orthodox work is felt to be a hindrance to the individual's realisation of his own potential. Both individuals felt they had to take drastic steps to alter the situation.

David Lloyd was riding high, holding a top position in an international company. Then aged forty-eight, he took the momentous decision to quit. There was no question of his career being on the decline, on the contrary he had just been offered further promotion and looked set to reach the very top. But the new post he was being offered meant a transfer to Switzerland, and this crystallized for him many of the nagging doubts he had been having as he approached midlife. His ties were essentially with England, and for him identity issues were intimately connected with his English past. A move to Switzerland would have meant distancing himself from this, perhaps irrevocably, as well as slotting into the designated role of his new post with its stronger sense of corporate identity. Much to his company's surprise he turned down their offer and set himself up as an independent consultant. His crisis was therefore self-induced, prompted by the searching demands of his psyche (Who am I? Where am I going? Where have I come from?).

Originally he came from a close-knit family where there 'was an unstated but inculcated parental drive to achieve', to be something special. As the only boy with two elder sisters he was sent off to a Public School tucked away in the country where he disliked the tribal, monastic atmosphere, the lack of sensitivity and general unacceptability of showing emotions. But for him the overriding factor was not to let his parents down. He felt 'a duty to them, to the investment they had made in my development and education.' This became converted to a sense of 'owing it to oneself', having to sustain a level of achievement and performance that was commensurate with these expectations. This loading of hopes onto him gave him a first taste of having to shoulder it all by himself and it left him feeling something of 'an individualist, an outsider, a rebel.'

He then went to Oxford University and into a career in advertising, 'a nice, broad, general, fairly sexy thing to do in the early sixties.' It was the business world with 'a slightly creative touch to it.' But after two to three years, he was ready to move – 'something said it wasn't really me.' Temporizing, he took up a post as tutor to a young twenty-year-old American from a prominent USA industrial family and accompanied him round Europe. They were, he feels, trying to 'buy something for their son which they as mother and father should have given him emotionally'. It told him something about the 'other' side of work, the focus on the educative, creative side that now interests him.

His next move was into economic consultancy and before long he was in a senior managerial position. As he was drawn more and more into the business world, he sensed that he was losing the chance to do anything more 'specialized and distinctive'. The urge for a creative outlet was always 'nagging away' but he felt he had to 'swim with the tide'.

'If people say when you're in your late twenties or early thirties "You know, David, I think you'd be very good at this or that, or why don't you take over our operation in Paris?' you're seduced by it, it's an exciting possibility.' He found many aspects of business to be creative; producing results was a bit like conducting an orchestra, and it wasn't long before he ended up as Chief Executive for the UK division of his international company.

His crunch point came in his mid forties when his company wanted him to run the whole of their international operations from Zürich, home of the parent company. The combination of having to sever his ties with England and stresses in his private life brought matters to a head.

I think too I was finding the whole thing meaningless. I had reached the stage of having a minor nervous breakdown around that time. It wasn't affecting my performance badly enough or they wouldn't have offered me the promotion. But inside I knew I'd lost an edge. I knew I was a bit burned out, questioning myself, my abilities, all those sorts of things – a loss of confidence, as often one gets at midlife. The high wire you have to walk along each day gets higher, there's no safety net. People are waiting for you to fall.

There is an undeniable loneliness to being at the top that is often under-recognized, an isolation for the king figure. He stands out from the rest of the group, and feels exposed, conscious of being looked at on his high wire, his performance constantly being judged. This exposure can lead to a sense of shame as surprising in its way as that more easily recognized in those who have failed, who have left the group by the lower exit. David Lloyd feels he took it upon himself to be in this 'lonely figure' position, 'to be the kind of animal that was different. It suited my temperament anyway' and, in part, stemmed from his family ethos and the pressure to succeed.

Being the only non-Swiss at that level of seniority, and knowing that he was 'head and shoulders above any other non-Swiss in the company' only reinforced his isolated status. Going across to Switzerland to become 'one of us', a corporation man, 'a member of the inner, inner club that wear our medals and wear our tribal costume', was more than he could take on. He didn't want to move to 'their home ground which I'm not part of, at ease with – it's not really my ball game.' He felt he needed to 'reject this whole way of life and get back to this deep-seated need to do something' and focus more on 'people and relationships'. He had reached the point where 'midlife in an adult sense is like someone blowing the whistle. Do I go on playing that game or do I now switch or play it a different way? Instead of becoming a player, I wanted to become a manager.'

He knew it was a risky decision to make. 'I was saying no.' Large international corporations do not like being turned down and he knew he was signing his own death warrant. Yet, surprisingly he found it a comfortable decision for him to make. It seemed right ('I had a good gut feeling about it') and he sensed that somehow this was the right move for him.

He consulted three of his closest friends for their advice and they supported his decision that if his heart was in England he should not go. The Swiss company didn't immediately say, 'Oh well you don't love us, we'll reject you.' They actually invited him a second time nine months later. He refused again, they clearly did not want to lose him and then they restructured the company to put him in charge of the whole of Europe. But the seed of discontent had already been sown, the wheels of midlife transformation were beginning to turn irreversibly. In reality he knew his staying on was no more than a holding operation. Sooner or later a 'young Turk' would be appointed to run the international side. There wouldn't be room for both of them. This happened and he gave in his resignation. 'I left with flags flying, all agreed. I left as a hero instead of yesterday's man.'

He moved into high-level consultancy taking on the psychological and career aspects of work as if the two sides of his nature previously underused could now be brought fully into operation. 'Most people have either a rational, logical way of doing things or have an artistic spark. The artists are bad at getting their act together and the doers are good at it.' Now by catering for both he was giving back some of his accumulated experience to others. 'In organizations, it's not the computer, it's the people and our franking-machine relationships with one another that mean we're really rather bad at communicating with one another. We all talk a lot but we don't listen enough, particularly chief executives.'

Part of his decision to withdraw was because his marriage was running out of steam and there were complications arising from a second relationship he had started up with a woman much younger than himself. These problems contributed to the 'minor nervous breakdown' he mentioned earlier. He had also reached fatherhood late, with young children. Fatherhood, he found, was a 'terribly worrying thing', another for his list of personal enquiry. With so many complications coming to a head in his private life, the next three years for him were a tremendous upheaval which meant giving up everything, his home, his job, his career. 'Christ knows where it's leading but it had to be done.' He was getting ready for a 'vast amount of midlife change' and preparing himself for a healing crisis. 'You can't go on playing Hamlet any more, you've now got to go on to Lear' (that is, accept a more tragic view of life). From his knowledge of opera he takes the image of himself as the Flying Dutchman forever roaming the seas. 'In the end I will be an outsider, drawn to a kind of life script to keep moving on like the Flying Dutchman. At the same time there is another part of me saying quite genuinely, "Please will someone give me peace and avoid this torment. You can surely be creative without being tormented."'

Having got his freedom he can see its drawbacks. 'You're entirely your own master now. You've worked it so that you've got free of everything, you have the financial security, but you're still screwing it up in a way, aren't you?'

He's in the middle stage of his identity crisis, the stage of uncertainty. Being on his own makes it at times even more difficult. Self-doubt inevitably creeps in. Having given up his career because at a deep level he was not sure that, for all his achievement, he really believed in himself, he now finds the path of self-discovery tough and at times lonely. He misses the company of others, the chance of 'having something to react against which was stimulating and exciting', that he had at work.

He is an example of someone living out his crisis. It is hard to predict an outcome.

I think the future could go either way, but I suppose I'm probably more optimistic. Most people retire between sixty and sixty-five and then start to die. The process takes ten years or whatever. I feel it is terribly important not to have this miserable period after you retire. I don't want ever to retire as such, I'd like an activity into my seventies. I wouldn't want to run down like my dad who just retired and vegetated. He died ten years ago and my mother, who was younger than him, died four years ago. She didn't have any interests once my father died, she just switched off. I'm determined not to make the same mistake. I've learnt that from the death of my parents. I don't want to be a dreary old depressing bore of a senile man in his seventies and eighties so people can say 'he's very perky still you know'.

With his interest in his own psychological make-up, he took the opportunity to talk to his mother in the last two years before she died, questioning her about his childhood, and found it a very valuable exercise for both of them.

He is still in his 'dark wood'. 'I suppose I'm moving in some sort of purposeful direction. The last three to four years have been very hard and tough for me, I'm both less confident in some ways and wiser at same time. It's been a decade of upheaval, and I'm still in it.' There is an underlying resilience and strength of character that permits him to take on these midlife challenges.

Hold on long enough, the weather will change. I'm a great believer in that. You've got to be doing something active. Your luck changes, the wind changes, relationships change. Somehow somebody knocks on the door. He recalls President Nixon: 'Never, ever, ever give up.'

The next story is of a more drawn-out search for identity, but as with the previous person the search is still going on.

Henry Bridges, now aged forty, was born in Jamaica, and has lived in London for over ten years. He first had a crisis aged twenty-nine when his first marriage split up. Now he is married for the second time, his wife coming from a Cambridge academic family.

Five years ago when he was thirty-five he faced an identity crisis. He realized he needed time out to reflect on where his life was going, explore his inner world, and link this up with his origins. Living in London, racial issues are never far away (in Lena Horne's phrase 'If you're black, you wake up political'). He went on a course at Surrey University at Guildford that allowed him to do this and it produced a second crisis of self-examination. He is still in the throes of this, in a state of uncertainty that is beginning to point him in the right direction. Recently he was forty, a key midlife point.

The fantasy I had for three years about my fortieth birthday was to ring up my sisters in Hartford, Connecticut and to say 'Leave supper for me' and then I'd get on Concorde. That was my fantasy. It wasn't to be. Probably I'll do it when I'm fifty.

I'm not sure what my feelings were about being forty. I think when I was twenty-nine, on the brink of my thirtieth birthday, that was a point in my life when I seemed to have a very strange feeling. I became very conscious about my age, it felt as if I was going over a kind of brink. For the first time in my life I became conscious about the future in terms of job security and financial security. I took out an Endowment Policy, which matures next year, so every time I see my bank statement and see the debits of terms of this thing, I remember being twenty-nine.

In 1979, I had recently emigrated from Jamaica and my first marriage was going through hell and was about to split up. Once it did split up there were questions like 'Where am I going now?' – 'What's the future?' I threw myself heavily into community work in East London. For two or three years it almost became a six-day-a-week occupation, and because I lived locally and people had my home number there'd be dreadful phone calls in the middle of the night and weekends and early mornings for a period of three or four years and I'd get very stressful in my relationships. I had several women friends but we never seemed to take relationships seriously at the time and I certainly didn't want to settle down. I think I felt a lot of my trust had sort of been betrayed because of the first marriage going wrong. I had a whale of a time because I was in the pub getting drunk at nights and on the other hand having lovely relationships with women friends, but nothing permanent – relationships in which I went feet in first and head in afterwards. I suppose the good thing about that period of my life is that gradually I came round to trusting friends again and building new relationships.

When I was thirty-five, I began to give up this six-day-a-week commitment. I was under a lot of pressure at work in East London with families and with the Rasta conflict in that community. Young black people were getting arrested by the police and there would be calls for help from parents and relations and so on. I don't think I realized at the time that I neglected my own needs, but I remember going into see my boss and said 'Look, I feel it is time that I have a bit of time for myself.' What I did was look around for what you might call a day release, and I ended up, in my thirty-fifth year, going to a two-year one-day-a-week course at Guildford doing humanistic psychology. I chose it as I needed some time for reflection; my brain cells needed to be stimulated again but I didn't want to do an academic course for the sake of pieces of paper.

So for two years I was going off to Guildford every Monday, which felt like bliss. Ok, I had to get across the traffic on to the A3 to Guildford, or sometimes a train, but it felt like bliss to be getting away from work. I was also doing a lot of weekend courses on Saturday and Sunday. Sometimes I stayed in Guildford and other times I travelled back. I did a lot of regression work which took me into some of my childhood experiences and formative relationships and I was astonished to see that there was so much hung over in terms of my relationship with my parents which is a severe pain. I went into some deep pieces of work to grapple with those early experiences and some of that pain which just got frozen and just never got talked through anywhere. I talked a lot about my father, I mean his whole attitude was the classic one of fathers who say 'I'm the boss around here and do as I say'. Out of that I realized that I was distrustful of men as well. That was interesting, but it wasn't surprising. It was the first time I realized that I suppose it had to do with some of the violence that was around my dad as well. Then I did some energetics themes with Gerda Boyesen and some work on psychosynthesis – integrating the mind on the body and psychic parts and so on.

I learned a lot on the course. I would say it has changed my life and I would say at the same time that it threw up a lot of issues and what seem to be unfinished pieces of work. The last four or five years have been one of crisis, extremely traumatic times when I've been extremely depressed. At Guildford I read whole books relating to some of those things I mentioned earlier and read a lot of stuff on astrology. I've also been doing a lot of dream analysis; working with my dreams and putting some of it on paper along with some bits of painting. It seems that the fundamental questions which were put to myself and others in the group – 'Who am I? What am I?' – in different words and in different ways are the questions that are still around.

The course helped Henry Bridges narrow his focus onto the question of identity, which took precedence at that time over work and relationship issues.

I think it is probably significant to say, as well, that the last ten years, and the last five years in particular, have constituted one of the last phases in my struggle to throw off the deep religious experience I grew up with which involved both the Baptist Church and the Christian faith. I thought that that was something I'd rejected thirteen to fifteen years ago, when I went to a theological seminary, was trained as a pastor, got ordained, did three years in the church and then I just couldn't face it – I just couldn't be part of that institution at all. The elders within the church told me that this was what God wanted me to do, not what I wanted to do, so I would say those ten years of my life were, in some ways, a total waste. There are a few things I take from that period of my life, some of the values associated with Christian faith (though these are not exclusive to Christianity) some of the values within my home and within the church, values I grew up with from a very young child. Those ten years ended up giving me the opportunity to be very critical. Even though it took ten whole years, I've worked through them intellectually and academically. So that is a plus I came out with, but I really regret in a way that that happened. I found a lot of the principles and ethics which the church stood for very questionable, and I found a lot of it oppressive. I left it consciously, believing I couldn't be any part of that hypocrisy and that oppression.

After I finished Guildford, I applied to London University, and I'm doing a course now in history and religious studies focused on Africa – part of it is an exploration into roots, and the African continent. I find I also want to establish this whole religious thread. I went to Egypt over the summer and visited a lot of museums, pyramids and ancient tombs. In Egypt, it was as if I were on some journey, on some kind of pilgrimage. I came back and it seemed emotionally that something had happened, as if I had changed between going away and coming back. One of the things I did in October was that I had a big bonfire in the back garden and I burnt all my ties; I had to burn an old hymn book as well, which I wasn't sure about doing but I had to burn something symbolically which represented my life in the Church and that oppressive experience.

I am not sure what all this represented, it may be something to do with my parents. I say that because – let me just divert for a little bit – before I went off to Egypt I had several dreams about my body being covered with beetles and I thought this was strange. I woke up several nights feeling sweaty and hot, and when I was in Egypt visiting the tombs I suddenly remembered the dreams. In a lot of these ancient tombs of Pharaohs and kings and nobles, the tomb walls are decorated in beeltes, or scarabs. There are scarabs everywhere in Egypt and I bought several. In one of the shops there was a man who spoke very good English so I was able to get into a conversation with him about the meaning of the scarab and he said the scarab represents life and one of the sayings about scarabs is that they have neither mother nor father. Now I came out the shop, kind of smiling, laughing because it seemed to me I had made a connection. My dreams then seemed to take on a new meaning and a new dimension and obviously my sub-conscious had been doing a lot of processing about how I feel with my parents and so on.

From questions relating to his own identity, he has been led on to discuss the personal significance for him of religion in his life. This is a two-way process: on the one hand it is a way of reconstructing his own religious past that was, he felt, imposed on him in his earlier years; and on the other hand it is a way of turning round this experience so that it has personal relevance to him, so that religion can provide a meaning to the second half of his life. This searching has also taken him into an understanding of his relationship with his father and the need to come out from under his shadow.

My parents celebrated fifty years of marriage on Boxing Day last year, and one of the things that was around through the year was whether I was going to go back for this celebration. So I went through this deep search of myself: 'Why do I want to go to Jamaica to celebrate my parents fiftieth wedding?'; 'It's nothing to do with me, it's not my wedding'. All these sort of statements were coming up when I was talking to myself. Two or three of my sisters in the States were planning to go down and there was talk of some kind of family reunion. Well, after Egypt and after processing that dream work and that experience about scarabs, I decided I wasn't going to go to Jamaica and it seemed to me I had to cut some kind of bond. They're still very close, but I think for the past ten years that I've been away they've been close in a pretty unhealthy way in the sense that I was caring too much for them and what's happening to their own lives in Jamaica. I think I cut something in that bond which relates to my parents.

Another part of the bond is the religious question. It's a fundamental question because there is a gap, a vacuum in my life. There's not a body of belief or ideology that I can practise anymore. A lot of times it feels as if it is a lonely journey that I'm walking because I've practically given up my job. I only do eight hours a week and most times it feels as if it's a job that I don't believe in anymore or that I've outgrown. It feels as if I want to move on and the question is 'move on to what' and of course I can't answer that, so that's kind of where I am at the moment. I'll probably wait till next summer when I've completed the course at college. Sometimes it feels as if I have no motivation at all to finish. I'll sit and read books from cover to cover, but the actual discipline of sitting down to write the work isn't always there.

This is the stage of uncertainty, of floating, half ridding himself of his past routines and habits, half uncertain whether to commit himself to the future. By completing the course he is committing himself to the unknown future. He recapitulates over the start of this midlife phase.

Something fundamental and significant was happening for me when I gave up a full-time job. I realized that I was giving, giving, giving and not giving anything to myself, or hardly anything. It was right to go to Guildford. The first year gave me the space and the break, while over the last year it sometimes feels as if now I have too much time to think, but perhaps there are questions around that I don't want to face, that I want to put off. There's always a question around about 'How do I fit in this society and where do I go from here?'

Henry Bridges even thought of going back to Jamaica which would 'allow me to be free in a way that I can't be in this country.' Having reduced his working life, he finds it hard to contemplate other jobs.

I've been pretty disillusioned with the jobs world, so I don't see a career in my line of work for the future because what I do changes nothing. Let me put it another way: the greatest disappointment and disillusionment with my sort of job is working with an organization that has limited resources and has no power politically. We've set up joint projects with the Local

Authority, i.e. youth centres for unemployed young people, but now they are all shutting them down, because of the cuts. It really depresses me, so I'm somewhat disillusioned. I don't want to go into Local Government because I would have to sit at a desk passing pieces of paper.

Despite the difficulties of being black and an immigrant he doesn't see 'the ten or fifteen years of living here as something I regret.'

There are lots of pluses, my vision has been expanded, hundredfold. Leaving Jamaica and living here has an advantage of looking out in the world through the media we have here and the access to information is phenomenal. I've learnt a lot. On the other side there have been struggles on a personal level and I can't, I'm afraid, side with the system. Part of the cause is that I can't at all accept what is happening in Local Government or Central Government. I think I am depressed because of what's happening politically, but at a personal level it's not so frightening. I mean, I know I have another year and a half at college and I want to stay with that, but I'm not sure what the long-term risk will be in two or three years time.

His sense of the future does not, at the moment, encompass having children.

I mean, it suits me fine, but I think I have a funny feeling that part of the reason I don't want children is tied up with my parents. I've often posed that question 'Why don't I want children and need children?' I think I've had paternal instincts sometimes and I watch myself with children and I can see that I'm very affectionate and warm and I've always been close to my nieces. In '83 we went home and my dad was asking whether we were going to have children and I said 'No' and he said 'Why not?' and I said 'Well the family is big enough.' So he said 'It's all well and good you talk about your brothers' and sisters' children but they're not yours.' I said 'Yes they're mine.' That was the conversation. But no, for us there aren't any pressures at all. And we feel that a lot of things we can do we would not be able to do if we had children – one of the bonuses – I don't know whether it's a selfish reason; it may well be. But I think that if we were both deep down desperate, we would have had.

His priority at the moment is to continue with his journey of self-discovery.

Looking ahead into the future, it feels as if I would want a little bit more time just to be. I have the feeling that when I've done all of that and spent three months lying on a beach, then I will get off my backside and there will be the feeling 'Right, I'm ready now to go.' I have the feeling it's

going to happen like that, that the energy will come back again; I think the
energy's gone and it probably will come back.

A friend of my wife who is a kind of spiritual guru and a kind of medium
sent me two paintings last year, inspirational portraits, that are not
planned but come to him in waves and vibrations and thoughts. One was
me in my previous life, and I was a stone-mason. It probably was right
because the last three years I've gone all over the place collecting stones. I
have stones that I collected in Newcastle, big stones, huge ones and the
stones I brought back from Egypt. Friends have gone off to India and I've
asked them to bring me stones back. I have one that came back from
Mauritius – stones from Malta – stones from Sudan – from all over the
place.

In broader philosophical terms he is still keeping an open mind.

I think to some of these questions, we have to say 'as far as we know, as far
as the knowledge we have'. We don't have enough knowledge to know
whether there is an after life. Certainly I don't accept the Christian
explanation of resurrection any more. I think it was Bertrand Russell
who, when asked what he would say if in the ultimate analysis he met God
and had to account for the fact that he had denied him and had been an
atheist, said he would say to God that he hadn't given him enough
information. So on the information I have, I don't think I believe in the
after life. I believe in this thing about cosmic consciousness though. There
seems to be something within the cosmic universe that seems to me to give
out energy – it's about harmony – it's about life – there's something out
there. I think I am at my most peaceful self, and my happy self to some
extent, when I'm in harmony with the universe. At other times when
there's a lot of trauma around I know it's a vibration that I'm picking up.

He defines his own sense of direction.

I think the purpose of the journey is about growth: it's about growing; it's
about growing and expanding and extending, emotionally and spiritually.
I think I could only say to some degree it's going to make me a better
person, a happier person; I don't think a better person in terms of
morality but I think a better person in terms of my capacity to love and be
loved and to give, and to love others. I think that is what that journey's
about. Makes me wiser too in terms of looking at the world. I think it's
making me more realistic about life and I think the greatest kind of
throw-me-down into the depression is part of the journey in life. I think
I'm also reluctantly and painfully, perhaps I don't want to admit it,
arriving at a stage where I'm going to have to accept that I can't change
the world and perhaps there is very little around me that I can change. I

think that is something that is taking place or unfolding itself within this journey, within this probe.

He's reaching a crucial midlife realization of his limited capacity to change the world, which is a step towards accepting the reality of his situation.

It's somewhat painful letting go. But I think part of not wanting to let go is tied up with the idea of letting go of hope, of accepting that one can't change things, that society is going to be what it is and people will continue to be selfish, and continue to be greedy, and continue to be violent.

I mean there is one difference to all of that and it is my own friends and loved ones who I know are not like that, not like those people. I think that is the thing that keeps me going, that is important. I can remember there are friends around that share the kind of perspective that I share, though we might not be able to change things.

I think I can accept the bits of me I don't like. I think it's easy enough to accept that because in a way I think the old frame of reference which was the religious/judgmental one no longer operates – that's gone – so I don't think I make those sort of judgments. I think I can live with myself. I can accept what I am.

You know, two years at Guildford was one of the best things that has happened to me in the last few years, because it made me start loving myself, caring for myself, not giving and giving and giving endlessly. The difficult part is, there are bits that I have to go back and work on in terms of Guildford – it feels like that – that's where the pain is I think. And sometimes it feels as if I know what I am about and what I'm searching for. At other times I don't think I know, so there's a sense of frustration and sense of search and a sense of probe going on.

One of the things I did at Guildford in our workshop involved a session where we all took our clothes off. I can't remember which particular exercise it was but we were only required to take off shirts and trousers and dresses and I was the one that requested in the group that we all strip off our clothes. I think, looking back, for me that was an experience . . . an experience to do with myself undressing before others. Apart from many years ago at school, or whatever, it had never happened, but I felt safe in that group. I must have done it for a reason at the time, I wasn't sure why, but it gave me a sense of freedom and sense of liberation.

I feel healthy, I feel Ok in my body. I'm lazy at the moment – I'm sleeping too much. I did take up some yoga last term and discovered that my body felt different. The tension which I carried around particularly in my back disappeared after yoga, so I learnt something important from that as well. Realizing that the tension had gone in my back made me reflect on some work with Gerda Boyesen. She had us lying down on the floor and observed that the middle of my back was some two inches off the floor. She did some work on my back and I suddenly remembered two experiences I'd had, one of which was crushing my fingers at school when a desk dropped on them. Her theory is about tensions which are carried in the back but which are not really to do with the back, but are sort of frozen experiences. The other experience had to do with the fact that I accidentally killed one of my cats when I was about twelve. I got into bed, rolled over, squashed it, woke up in the morning and there was this cold thing under my back and then I discovered it was my kitten. It was when I was in Guildford I realized that the posture I had in my back caused some of the tensions and pains I was carrying. Those two pieces of work helped me to release that, so I want to do some more yoga, it could do a lot more for me, spiritually, fundamentally, it could really lift up a lot of energy, so that is something I want to probe some more.

I was downstairs reading about 1 o'clock in the morning and doing this kind of review of my life, when these words came out on paper. I spent the first eighteen years of my life pleasing my parents and pleasing God; the next eighteen years pleasing others and working on personal relationships; but I was going to spend the next forty for myself. I'll leave you with that.

Henry Bridges is still very much on a journey of self-discovery; he leaves himself open to new experiences, and is waiting for the 'right moment' to happen. His quest for a surer sense of his own identity is now well on its way.

5

Marital Discord

The fundamental trouble with marriage is that it shakes a man's confidence in himself, and so greatly diminishes his general competence and effectiveness. His habit of mind becomes that of a commander who has lost a decisive and calamitous battle. He never quite trusts himself thereafter.

H L MENCKEN

Woe to the house where the hen crows and the rooster keeps still.

SPANISH PROVERB

Along with work and resolving identity issues, marriage is the third area for precipitating major midlife changes. Midlife can be the doldrums of married life or the chance for it to take off into a new lease of life. Pressures are felt by both partners. The classic male example is the husband who flies the coop, going off with a younger woman in search of renewal and rejuvenation. If he's just seeking to recapture his adolescence, the search will be in vain. He'll be avoiding dealing with his own identity crisis at midlife or acknowledging the changes required within his marriage.

Midlife accentuates the sense of growing old with its feared loss of vitality and this last fling mentality (or closing door syndrome, *torschlusspanik* in German) may be an attempt by the man to get away from the feeling that the young in him is being crushed by the old. Other men, prompted by the emergence of a 'feminine side' to their nature, may seek to contact this more through relationships with other women. The pop celebrity Sting commented recently, 'Part of my belief of what maturity is for a man is accepting that part of your psychological make-up is feminine. Now that involves really sorting out your relationship with your mother, which I think has a direct effect on your relationships with women for all time: girl friends, wives, daughters, mistresses, whatever.' Midlife revives some of the forgotten effects of the maternal relationship, as a man is released from some of the pressures of work and breadwinning and comes to rely more on his wife.

Midlife marks for many marriages the beginning of the post-parental years when the children have left, or are about to leave, home. The marriage partners find themselves on their own again, perhaps for the first time in twenty years, and inevitably come to re-assess their relationship with one another. The discomfort of such a state can produce unexpected side effects. A couple may easily project onto each other individual 'faults'. A husband may 'discover' all sort of flaws and shortcomings in his wife that properly belong to him and the situation he is in, and may accuse her of being inconsiderate, uncaring when these are the qualities he's hesitant to 'discover' in himself. He may delude himself into believing that he has missed noticing these 'defects' in his wife over the years.

His wife is now found wanting in sex appeal, intelligence, social *savoir faire*. The lack of excitement between them is put down to her failure to share his main interests and concerns. It is all her fault – whereas the crisis and distress at this juncture properly belong to him. Lines of communication get stretched, even broken. Off-loading criticism, accusing each other of shortcomings are ways of defending oneself against the need to change. The 'hidden' conflict of the marriage is brought into the open, having been damped down over the years by the pact of compatibility required to bring up children, and by the habit-forming rhythm and routine of family life, and the inertia this often produces. Midlife with its explosive changes can unbalance these routines and cause marriage partners to wonder exactly what this original pact was based on.

A precipitating factor for crisis is often the changed position of the wife within the marriage. The wife, if children have left home, may now wish to free herself from the shackles of domesticity and begin to develop her own interests, particularly outside the home. The husband, on the other hand, if he is no longer sustained by the illusion of job advancement nor reinforced in his role as parent, feels under threat; his 'ascendancy' at home on which he relies for a good deal of his self-esteem is being challenged and he may have always used this to bolster his shaky self-esteem at work. As the balance swings the other way, and the wife detaches herself more from home and her subordinate role there, the husband is left facing a personal crisis. He may long for a return to the *status quo*, or at least for a continuation of life as it now is.

A marriage can sort itself out, through openness and discussion (a 'fair fight'). Men have an extra responsibility at this time to acknowledge what is going on in their marital relationships; to question and understand what their dependence is about; and to ask themselves why, to some extent, they are reluctant to form more adult relationships with women. At this point many men are resistant to change, nor do they, fundamentally, want their wives to branch out on their own.

Containment, which is at the heart of a successful marriage, now has a double-edged meaning: it can either become defensive and counter-productive, warding off the anxieties and fears of both partners; or it can move the marriage a stage forward providing a safety net for development to take place. A marriage that sees itself as concerned with psychological development rather than making sure it avoids psychological pain, will be able to cope with these sorts of stresses. After all, midlife is about change. In two of the stories that follow it is the wives who have taken the initiative to alter the status of the marriage. Indeed this is generally the pattern. The husbands in these cases seem to have been too preoccupied with external concerns, the pursuit of career, to notice fully what is happening at home. The wife, having repressed her instincts over the years, may demand more out of life. She will actively seek out a life or career for herself outside the home, and expand her horizons.

The husband, while on the surface encouraging this, may secretly resent it, and feel threatened by his wife's 'liberation'. Deep down he would much prefer to hold on to the situation he has always known – his wife as a steady, constant, reliable companion – especially if he is going through a shaky time himself. He may be hoping for extra support from her. He may be floundering around, the child-in-the-man now making its unseasonal appearance and bringing to the forefront primitive, long-forgotten fears of abandonment. He is likely to keep up his demands at the same level. The wife may rightly refuse to fall in with this, which will then be experienced by the husband as a rebuff. Feeling belittled, humiliated or over-controlled, rather than ask himself why, he may go off in search of a better source of comfort. Finding a more sympathetic understanding with another woman seems to him to be a justifiable solution, but it is really an avoidance of his responsibilities at this stage, and of recognizing that he is in the throes of midlife upheaval.

Effectively what may often be happening at midlife is that there is a crossover of roles, husband and wife each taking up more of the other's psychological stance. Each sex becomes more of what the other used to be, the husband becoming more dependent and deferential and the wife more aggressive and managerial. Both sets of characteristics may well have been suppressed during the preceding period of parenthood. The husband's primary concern to secure the material well-being of the home, may have meant he has missed out on demonstrating his capacity for intimacy, while the wife may have submerged her aggressive side for fear of the emotional damage it might do to her children. Each has voluntarily given up parts of themselves in the service of child-rearing. Once this is over, these repressed feelings can be allowed out and expressed. Men may find a suitable outlet for their feelings of concern and relatedness in some form of 'generativity' while women may seek out some form of 'executive' power to release their organizing abilities and competitive instincts. The worst outcome is when no suitable outlet is found and couples become engrossed in excessive self-absorption, a form of stagnation where each partner becomes the other's 'infant and pet', and days are spent preoccupied by hypochondria, pettiness and irritability.

Some marriages simply run out of steam at midlife. When couples feel they have outgrown each other, the 'hidden conflict' reveals that the marriage wasn't properly grounded. They may have married due to family pressure, or for money or to improve their social position. The high divorce rate is proof enough of the lack of staying power of nearly one in three marriages. But most marriages do survive and weather the crisis of midlife, seeing it as a time for acceptance of loss and gain and a re-working of the existing text. Such an undertaking is almost sure to strengthen a marriage, and lead to greater understanding, bringing its rewards in closeness and companionship through old age.

Edward and Lisa married young when both were at university. Their first child was born soon afterwards. The early years of marriage were contented, though money was often short. By the time they had reached their mid-thirties the marriage came under a lot of pressure. Their children had grown up. There was a feeling around that they wanted to catch up on what they had missed out on by getting married so young. Each embarked on extra-marital affairs, and it looked as though the marriage was heading for the rocks. Accusations and counter-accusations flew across the breakfast table. Who had sacrificed more for the other, who was entitled to what and, crucially, who would be looking after whom? This phase lasted some two to three years. But it was a marriage where tensions were brought out into the open, the partners went on talking to each other and the unsettling period was survived. The attempts to shake the foundations of the marriage were seen for what they were, a temporary but necessary aberration. The marriage was restored, and a stronger, more trusting bond established between them as partners.

Increasingly, we find that midlife and the prospect of change are seen often as enemies, or at least as a threat. Yet without change there is no progress. Jung has a phrase that 'if you're not interested in your fate, then your unconscious is'. Never is this truer than at midlife and in the first story Tony Gibson lets 'fate' take a hand in deciding his future.

Tony Gibson spoke to us five weeks after he had moved into a new house in Essex with his girl friend Jane. He has always been keen on houses and was relishing the novelty of this one, built of new materials round the courtyard of an existing large nineteenth-century house. Things are now looking up for him and he looks forward to a future lined with several possibilities. He's a well-built man, with curling grey hair (unusually long for a policeman) and he looks younger than his forty-six years. There is a coiled watchfulness about him, which may be to do with his work as an Inspector in the police force, and the habit of observation that's part of that job. He starts by describing his daily life as a policeman and its effect on his home life.

At work there are times when I show compassion and times when I've got to be as hard as iron. I get up and leave it and come home and I'm me. I never bring any of my uniform home, other than shirts to wash. I go to work and strip down to my socks and pants, change and adopt a new role. I mean, the neighbours know I'm a policeman and if they've got a problem I'll advise them or help them but apart from that I don't want to know. I'm not looking at tax discs on the car and that sort of thing. I leave work at work, come home and spend that first hour and a half unwinding, releasing it. That's why I deliberately live away from work. We could have chosen a house nearer but I like the idea of coming away. It's so different from the working environment.

I prefer people to know me as Tony, other than as a policeman. You go to a party and everything stops 'Here's a copper'. I quite deliberately lie on holiday so that I get two weeks of enjoyment. At the end of it, if I feel I'm still going to keep in touch, I say 'Well I'm not . . . I'm so and so, but now you've spent two weeks with me, you know I'm not the "image".' I don't feel that I fit into the characterization of the policeman anyway. OK, I might look the part, being quite tall, but that's just the way I have to be. I've had hair down the middle of my back and a long beard. I've been different at other times in my life. I just have to conform at the moment. I go to Open University and people don't know what I do, at their summer schools I tell them I'm a lorry driver, you know, and I thoroughly enjoy myself. And I sit there and there are maybe one or two policemen – I can pick them out a mile, that's the funny thing. And they get so much hassle and stick and people think me totally different and that amuses me, so yes, I don't say I hide from it. If something happened I'd be out there like a shot and deal with it, but it does restrict you socially and people have so much of an image and they think you've got to be like that. You haven't got to be like that at all.

He and his present girl friend are both police officers, working at the same station. Their shifts often follow one another which means they get very little time together.

Jane's going in now at 2 o'clock and she finishes at 10 tonight and hands over to me. I take over and finish at 6 o'clock tomorrow morning. So that's a difficulty, I come home and she's in bed asleep. We won't see each other now until probably about Tuesday or Wednesday next week, so it does present problems. But within a month that should sort itself out, because we've now said openly 'We're now about to live together' and they've decided that we should not be doing the same job, so Jane's got another job elsewhere, possibly at Scotland Yard and in fact I probably will do some teaching. We could both end up with normal hours which will be quite nice. At the moment it's quite difficult finding time for each other really.

They have known each other for eighteen months and had been seriously seeing each other for twelve months. They each had their own properties before they decided to sell them both and buy this one jointly. They are waiting for her divorce to come through. Tony takes up the story.

I'd been separated for four and a half years and got divorced eighteen months ago now, so I wasn't in any particular rush to enter another relationship and make a mistake. I was happy to just let things evolve, so that's how we've come here together and put the two homes into one. We were discussing in the car this morning the amount of emotional stress over the last eighteen months. There's been quite a lot on both of us really. Fortunately I was divorced so I could help her through and say 'Well he's reacting because of so and so' and I can understand why and explain it to her saying 'Don't worry, don't react, just let it be'. So from that point of view perhaps it's helped that both break-ups hadn't been going on at the same time. Mine was out of the way.

I've lived on my own for four and a half years, virtually in one room – rented accommodation up until a year ago. I've missed having a family and children about, no matter what age. Mine are grown up now. Both are boys – I'd always wanted a little girl, a daughter, so I'm lucky there – got a ready-made one now (Jane has a daughter aged four). I enjoy looking after her, many times over the last six months I've looked after her from breakfast to putting her to bed.

I was married for nineteen years and was twenty-one when I got married. My first wife was also a police officer. She left to have the children, who came along very quickly, after three or four years. She stayed at home looking after them and by the time the younger was into school, tenish, she decided she wanted to re-take a career, which is fine. She'd been at home fourteen years and she decided she wanted to go into social work, so she did three years college as a mature student and then got a job and then had an affair with someone at work. It was difficult for me to cope with. It was the sort of position that he was twelve years younger than her. I found the competition quite difficult and began to resent it feeling 'Why do I need to compete?' It was just a phase. I don't think I could come to terms with it. Nothing seemed to go right after that. I'd always been pretty handy in the home, cooking and washing and ironing, because we were both doing full-time jobs and I'm quite happy to do the washing, ironing and shopping, that sort of thing. And in fact because of my hours at the time I often used to have a meal ready for her when she came in.

She often didn't get back until about 6.30 at night. What she was doing, I don't know. But when she came home at 6.30 there was a meal. It suddenly got to the stage where I felt . . . well, in fact I went to Marriage Guidance, and to my surprise the guidance turned out to be: 'Well, what are you doing – you're being used really. Is it what you want?' I then decided to make plans to leave and sort out something. It got to the stage one day when I just picked up a carrier bag and put some clothes into it and drove to the end of the road. Got to the end of the road and didn't know whether to go left or right, you know. I hadn't really planned it at all. I started living in spare rooms in people's houses for a while, until I got myself sorted out.

It was a surprise to my children when I left because I don't think they knew. I didn't tell them anyway. They didn't know my wife had been having an affair or what the reasons were. It was suddenly Dad packing a carrier bag and leaving, so it hit them very hard. They were in their teens, to me it was probably the most important time when I should be there to control them and also guide them through quite a difficult period in their lives. I felt very guilty about going at that particular time. The younger one, I had lots of problems with, he just wouldn't talk to me on the phone and I had very little contact in person with them because my wife was keeping them round her and not allowing me into the house and that sort of thing. And it took a long time, probably a year, before things improved. The older one was easier and spent more time with me. Then as time went by, no problem, with both of them.

Eventually things got better. I went through a stage of going to a pub every night for company. I decided that wasn't any good, so I then took up Open University and am now into my fifth paper. Having had a large house and a family, suddenly to switch to one room (no decorating problems, no gardening) left me with such a lot of time. Going down the pub wasn't the answer, so I sorted myself out and did something I wanted to do. History for the last four years and I'm doing Renaissance Art in France this year. It's totally different to what I do at work, you know. It's probably more me actually, frustrated artist at heart.

This floating existence served its purpose. It allowed him to separate from his immediate past and discover new horizons for himself, living a temporarily unattached existence with minimal possessions before discovering his true path again. Art was something he had first thought of as a career when young. He had got a scholarship to Ealing Art College but his step-father had advised against it. 'No money in art.' Now, his crisis lived through, he's considering going back to art college when he retires in about three years

time. It's part of his new-found quest for creativity. He points to a drawing in charcoal on the wall that he's recently done. 'I dabble at anything. I just do bits and pieces. I like these sort of techniques. I suppose I should go along to evening classes and things like that. I probably will.' His younger son is at Art College. 'He's doing what I didn't do. He keeps showing me all the bits and saying "Dad, you really should do it because you'll enjoy it." He's the one that's encouraging me to go back, or back in time.'

Is there a hint of envy here? It doesn't look like it, perhaps it's more a case of role reversal, of parenting the parents. Here the son is living the unlived life of his father.

I didn't think I was going to settle down again. I thought I'd sort of play the field for a while, but basically I'm a very domesticated person really. In a sense I began to think, 'Well, am I fighting back, am I taking revenge on the female?' I had a number of relationships that lasted no more than twelve months but they weren't the right people for me for various reasons. Maybe I wasn't ready then really, but from the time of going out with Jane, that was it, things seemed to slot into place. From that point on, I didn't play the field, but previously I'd had perhaps two or three at the same time. It was really my first freedom since being younger.

The middle phase of his crisis was to experiment, to try out new ways of living, and as often happens to catch up on the missed chances of early adulthood.

During the marriage, I hadn't messed around at all. I hadn't really thought 'How am I to other women?' I've always been a bit cold, you know, especially in a working environment. Work is one thing and I just didn't socialize. It wasn't a question of taking anyone out for lunch or anything like that. I just didn't at all and in fact the Marriage Guidance Counsellor said 'You've got to get over that complete barrier that you seem to have.' They were trying to make me stop being so stand-offish and keeping my distance. I suppose when I did eventually leave the marriage, I went too much the other way, and I suddenly realized in my forties I was still acceptable to a number of women, and that surprised me a little because I hadn't really thought of myself in that way. It did my ego some good. I started watching my weight and changed the clothes I wore.

Later to re-establish himself and give a solid base to his new outlook on life, he bought a new house.

It was a brand new house. I watched it grow from the foundations, landscaped the garden, moving quite a lot of earth about, built walls and rockeries and patios, planted trees and established quite a nice garden. I planned the whole of the house inside before I actually moved into it. So on moving in, everything was as I wanted it. I hadn't consulted anybody else at all because it was my house and it was going to be solely mine. I moved in two days before Christmas. Then I went out with Jane for the first time about a month later.

Perhaps there was a connection. He was now 'ready' for a proper relationship. 'Then suddenly I was going out with somebody and it began to get serious, and it threw me a little bit.' But he wasn't going to let his momentary discomfort stand in his way.

I decided that nothing should be sacred. She shouldn't come into my house and live in my environment because it wouldn't be fair on her. I said 'Let's create something else.' Ok, let's put all her things and my things together and say 'Do we both like it?' And that's what we've done. We've virtually gone through things. Some things I've put aside for jumble sales that had memories for me, but she might have done the same with things that she wanted too. So I think both of us have been aware of not wanting to have a dominant interest over the other person avoiding the 'this is all mine' and 'this is how its going to be' mentality. If we don't like something, we're honest with each other.

But there are still one or two difficulties left over from the past.

Since leaving my marriage I've experienced emotional problems and occasional sexual difficulties. I went to hospital to try to work it through and reason it out. We decided that one of the things I should do is more creativity. It hasn't totally resolved it; it's easier and it is getting better but it hasn't totally cleared. My fear was that if we came to live together Jane might be a bit resentful. I didn't want her to feel that because it wasn't her fault, it was something that was reacting within me, you know, that I couldn't release. I wouldn't let my true feelings go perhaps, and I was going back to this 'arms distance' bit that I've had with women in the past. 'Don't come near me, you might affect me, you might bug me, you might want something from me.' So at the moment I'm having slight problems but we talked it through and decided just to give it time and patience. We are both caring people and that was a new experience for me. My wife hadn't been at all demonstrative. She would never throw her arms round me, even making love, she would never just touch me, and I found that most peculiar. Jane enjoys touching and I find that very good and it's helping. I'm relaxing and unwinding, yes, it's coming back.

He's looking forward to his new job, as an outlet for his creative side.

What I'm going to be doing is on the teaching and training side. It's something new, something different. I'm not very good on public speaking and I'm going to have to do quite a lot of that – lessons and classroom work, that sort of thing – it would be a new challenge for me. It's creativity in a slightly different way; I have to write articles and things and I suppose a lesson can be boring or it can be good, so I can adjust a little bit there, but no, my creativity at the moment is still a learning process. As I say, I have to find time for myself and Jane is very aware of that because that is one of the things that came out of the counselling we got. It's Ok being a very caring person but sometimes you've got to think about your own needs and I'm aware of her needs, she wants to go to university and do things like that. We've discussed it and she'd be working in a very male environment. She's an attractive woman and I can't spend all my life on tenterhooks 'Is it going to happen again?' I couldn't live like that. I've got to trust her and she's got to trust me. If it's something she wants to do, I'm not going to suppress it.

His thoughts are turning to the future with retirement not that far away.

I've got to stay in the London area because Jane's going to be working in London for the next few years. If I work for myself, that would give us flexibility: if it's raining, I can go to work; if it's sunny, I can play golf or paint. I don't have to earn a tremendous amount because I've got a reasonable pension coming in. I thought of becoming a cab driver with a black cab as something that you can pick up and put down, take a month off or whatever if you own your cab. Get up at 6 in the morning and Jane says 'Pick me up at 5.30 tonight' that's fine. If she says 'Take two or three days off this week' and we'll go with her daughter to the coast, we can do that. If I am going to art college, it's something I can do at week-ends, at half-term or in the summer holidays and still bring in some pennies. So it's got a number of advantages for me. So I'm thinking of doing that as a long-stop, to avoid putting any financial burden on us. It takes two years to do the knowledge bit, two years in spare time it takes, just learning all those streets. In London alone there are 700 squares and then you've got to learn all the Embassies. It may take two years but the rewards are that you can go out and drive for twelve hours if you want to.

On reflection he feels excited about this new life that's opened up, though he acknowledges a sadness 'that things didn't turn out as I originally hoped. But I'm very aware that you can't sit and mope, you know. There's a time to pick yourself, dust yourself off and start again. I'm very excited.' They've discussed marriage:

. . . but the difficulty is, to my mind that it's like a bereavement: how soon after divorce do you marry? So we're looking at twelve months, this time next year, that's the sort of time. We're happy enough to know the direction we want to go in. I've been very fortunate that I'm at a very exciting period in my life, and free enough and able enough to do the things that perhaps frustratedly I've not been able to for such a long time. It's all coming together and I'm looking forward to it. The thought of actually going to college and competing against twenty-year-olds – Ok, give it a run, see how we go.

The next story describes a move from an unhappy marriage to one that is fulfilling. A full-scale midlife crisis lay between. Henry King had been a politician, with a period of ministerial responsibility, and now works as Managing Director of a business which he set up prior to becoming an MP. His crisis occurred in 1979 when three factors combined: he lost his seat as an MP; his marriage broke up; and he had to restart a career in business. His crisis may have been on the cards in any event: 'I was looking for it to happen actually in a way. I mean, without realizing what I was doing I was almost out of control.' He starts by describing his family background.

I was an only child and my mother invested a lot of hope in me. My father and mother didn't get along and I remember sort of being dragged out of the house with the luggage in one hand and me in the other leaving my father – early childhood memories. My father was a delightful man, they just should not have been married. He was a very kind, soft man and she was a tough lady, my mother, you know capable type, warm, much too able for him and she ran a shop and ran a garage and did all sorts of things like that. She was therefore in a classic situation: investing a lot in me as her only son who proceeded to do extremely well (you know, go to university, become a MP and all that sort of stuff) and then suddenly *clack*, you know, her marriage was failing.

An only child, carrying the full weight of parental expectations, his mother's pressure on him to succeed has been an underlying force in his life.

My father worked most of his life on the assembly line at Leyland Motors. He was just an ordinary fitter on the line. During the war my grandfather, my father's father, who was quite a rich man and was the local Conservative Mayor set up my father and his wife with a garage. But it rapidly became apparent my father was no businessman and my mother was. Also he had to go into war work. He couldn't fight, as he was blind in one eye and deaf in one ear. She ran the garage but when he came back – he was fascinated by cars and all that and terribly good with his hands – he had no business head at all. He'd give the petrol away he was so kind-hearted, and she couldn't stand that, so she packed it all up and bought a shop, because she could run a shop and manage the whole thing and be in control. He went to work in Leyland Motors and worked there for the rest of his life.

He died in the winter of discontent in '78, terrible winter. I was in Parliament then, all those bloody strikes. There was terrible weather and my father was dying in hospital with brain damage. Terrible time. I think my mother suffers great remorse because she was very irritable and fed up with him, because he was totally unambitious but he was a very moving man, and everyone loved him, and she loved him really. He was a perfect gentleman; he was an old-fashioned one who took off his hat to ladies and walked on the outside of pavements and always had a bag of sweets in his pockets to give to kids and he was just a sort of very gentle man, you know. He had a severe accident when he was in his twenties and nobody knew it. He just went on his motorbike into a lamp-post head first and he was in a coma for about nine months and he nearly died and nobody knew it but he had damaged his brain to a point where half of it didn't exist and he had this terrible do when he went in for brain surgery and cysts were developing and he had a terrible series of operations on his brain. It was the reason why he was slightly malfunctioning on one side of his head all of his life but it didn't affect his personality. Apparently, it's astonishing he lived his entire life with half a brain. He was a medical marvel actually. Maybe it can explain why he was a bit slow and a bit soft and wouldn't take responsibility and so on, and used to drive my mother barmy but we didn't know that of course.

It had its effect on Henry as his son. However attached he was to his father, he couldn't use him as a model in line with his own aspirations. As he began to make his way in the world after leaving university, he looked to marriage to give himself a prop but it was the wrong choice ultimately for him.

I got married to a woman several years older than myself, which was a mistake, although we loved each other dearly at the time and it was very romantic. I mean, I was in my twenties and she was several years older. After a wonderful initial period, it rapidly went wrong. It made me very unhappy and her very unhappy as well. They were probably simple problems and there are ways of solving problems these days but she was against getting help. I was in Parliament at the time and I was really very pressed, working like the clappers and doing ridiculous things like working until four o'clock in the morning in the House of Commons and then starting at nine o'clock having had three hours sleep or something. She was living in the country, so there were three effects: (a) I was working like hell; (b) we were living apart during the week; and (c) as a result of that sex deteriorated.

Then I lost my seat in the election and was coming back to the company I'd started as Managing Director very much on test as I hadn't done it for some years – they'd say 'What does he know about business?'. So that was, if you like, a classic middle-life sort of adjustment. I didn't realize what pressures were on me. The woman who helped me totally in that period, I'll never be able to thank her enough, was a psychotherapist, Mrs H. I mean I was riddled by guilt. I just felt that I was behaving awfully and I didn't know how to get out of this weight of guilt. I felt it was a total conflict between what I wanted and my obligations as a married man – I'd never been unfaithful before, I'm not an unfaithful sort of chap, I just don't believe in all that. And, you know, I had pretensions to being a moral person, and here I was being unfaithful. It was a curious coincidence. I had a health check-up and the doctor who saw me said 'You're under a bit of stress.' I explained it and he said 'Well, I'm a doctor, and I've just remarried my first wife. Seven years we were apart and it's all due to this remarkable Mrs H. I'll give you her telephone number.' So I phoned her up. I thought I should see somebody so I went to see her and her advice to me was absolutely clear-cut. She said 'You know, it's life or death. You should leave.' And it was a tremendous, you know, release. The joke is that a therapist tells you to do what you want to do anyway, it's almost licensed bad behaviour.

I was having great difficulty and was in a very stressful situation and the marriage therapist just gave me the push at the right time in the right place. I left my wife and I was living by myself in London, battered by this, trying to run a company, trying to pick up the pieces, and Mrs H. just gave me the extra bit of encouragement to carry on the course that I'd already embarked on and not to give up.

As for the future, my plan – one should be wary of plans – is to get back into Parliament and be part time here and part time in the House of Commons and tackle the whole thing in a different way. I'm less single-minded than when I was young. I've learned from that, and that's the understanding I have with the Chairman of my company. If I get back into the House I do mornings here and then go at lunch-time to the House, and thereby I'm able to get the best of both worlds. I've built up a group of people who can actually run the company without any difficulty, so I will carry on running this company until I see what happens between now and the next General Election – see whether I get a seat or not. If I don't get a seat, don't get a constituency, I might have to revise the whole plan and then try and do something else.

He's beginning to think of his responsibilities towards his mother now that she is ageing and may have to be looked after, rather than continuing to live on her own.

My mother still lives in the north, she's very happy I think. She's got a nice flat, it's near the Church where she spends all her social life. She can walk up the street in the summer, sit in the park and listen to the band.

Actually we were just discussing it this weekend. They're building blocks of flats literally next door to her present flat, which is for people over sixty and has all the things, you know, alarms bells and that sort of that stuff. They have one sitting-room, a bedroom, a kitchen and bathroom and I was just thinking it would be ideal for her. She's appalled by the price but I know that the prices really are not bad and unless we get in quick, we'll lose that, so that I think would be suitable for her. She's seventy-six now so another seven or eight years and she would be best in that situation. I mean we've obviously thought about bringing her down to London but I think it would totally cut her off from her friends and neighbours and local life.

Henry King has re-married and also acquired step-children, to whom he is close and who give him the sense of family that he's missed out on until now.

I'd never really wanted children very much, I'd always been far too single-minded about my career and all that – in retrospect wrongly. I've always been in far too much of a rush to get on and never paid enough attention to emotional private life when I was young. I mean, my first wife once said to me 'You never really married at all; you were married to me but never really married. You just behaved like a bachelor.' I didn't used to go out with other women but I behaved as a free man as it it were. I could do what I wanted to do. When I was in my twenties and early thirties I spent each weekend working because you have to outwork the others, but now I don't do that at all, quite the reverse. I don't work so hard now. I'm conscious of that. I do the politics which takes a certain amount of time (the odd weekend and evening and so on but I try as far as possible to get it all into the working day); and then I have evenings and weekends completely free to do the second thing – a lot of living: a lovely London life with opera (my wife has got a degree in music and is a great lover of music), theatre, films, golf, squash, jogging, weekends in the country. You know I really am enjoying life. Very selfish.

Having been through a considerable upheaval at midlife, he's beginning to wonder what lies ahead at the other end of life. He's not a particularly religious person.

I went to a non-conformist school where we went to chapel twice a day. I loved the hymns and the general atmosphere but when I left school I never went to church again, other than for weddings and funerals. So one wonders a bit about what's going to happen when you die and I just think it's the end. It's an appalling thought in a way. But I think as one gets older, one gets used to it and may even welcome it, because bodily functions change, and you adjust psychologically and physically more to dying. Then when it comes, it won't be as appalling as it seems today.

My own health is very good, fortunately. I mean that is a tremendous blessing, I'm so grateful for that. People I feel most unhappy for are the people who've never had proper facilities. The deaf, blind and mute and people who've had terrible accidents. Probably I have a horror of physical mutilation, having been spared the difficulties my father had. And all my family have lived to ripe old ages – they're all in their eighties and so forth, so I hope to do the same. By then I'll be reconciled to the fact that I'm about to die and that will be the end of it all.

Having spent the first half of life establishing himself in the world, meeting others' and his own expectations, he is closer now to reflecting on family ties. His appreciation of his father for all his 'weakness', shows how he, as a son, is tacitly acknowledging his presence in him and his debt to him.

It's remarkable to me how much one stays the same and also how much one changes, reverting to what one's family is like. I now see more of my relatives, more of my family in me, than I did and more of my father in me, and my mother in me than I have done hitherto. I'm less of a totally independent being, more the child of my parents and my family. I see the ambitious mother in me, occasionally thoughtless and hurtful (as I am to other people occasionally) and I see the kind father. I think that I've got a different view on ambition now. I've got it sensibly in perspective for the first time. Success is not only about my political career and all that, it's about what I've got: a happy relationship, trying to do things on the back of that, as it were; trying to run a business and be a responsible parent and do things well and effectively.

I mean the experience of my life, really, is that I went into politics too young, was too academically theoretical, left politics, started a business, realized that you've got to take tough decisions, and that there's no way you can pussy-foot around. If you do take tough decisions, things will come out right and people will thank you. If you don't take tough decisions, people just blame you. You can't care too much, otherwise you don't take the right decisions.

My mother took a tough decision sending me away to school because it meant she had nobody at home, that was a tough decision which she thought was right, because she thought that I needed a good male influence on me and my father wasn't that male influence in life. I was an only child and had to go away to a boys' boarding school and be surrounded by 'chaps' and get the right amount of masculine influence in my life which she couldn't give me. That was her tough decision.

Midlife for him has been a staging post, forcing him to put questions to himself about what he has achieved so far, how well or otherwise he has conducted his personal relationships, and what lies ahead for him. You get the feeling he will go on exploring. This interview caught him at the moment of post-crisis, at the resolution stage, having experienced his years of real difficulty. His strength lay in his ability to avail himself of resources around him, for example, the psychotherapist who appeared at a crucial transitional phase. Now he has got the balance between work and leisure right for himself and allows him to say with pride, 'I would say that last year was the happiest year of my life. I think that I'm sexually and maritally extremely happy. It all came right even though the scar is there. To live in London and live twenty minutes from work and to be home in the evenings and week-ends and be happily married – it's like bliss to me; I can't believe it happened to me.'

> The invisible worm
> That flies in the night,
> In the howling storm,
> Has found out thy bed
> Of crimson joy;
> And his dark secret love
> Doth thy life destroy.
>   William Blake

'Where are you living now?'
'With my parents – just round the corner.'

Graham Turner is forty years old. No, he is not a mamma's boy, who has never left home. On the contrary, he has been and still is a successful international banker; but he has been through a sudden and, for him, unexpected marital crisis. Now back home where he started, he faces the same questions as an adolescent; Who am I? Where am I going?

Three months ago his wife walked out on him. It was a classic case of 'I woke up one morning at forty, and my wife had left. My world had fallen apart.' No warning, no premonition on his part. Six months previously, they had been having the house redecorated, in keeping with their rising standard of living. The decorator and his wife got together. Fifth column, trouble within, enemy within the gates.

As a banker, Graham is in charge of foreign exchange control, a senior and important position. He is used to making decisions, taking the long view, getting things to fit the overall scheme. Maybe he applied this to his marriage. Had he been too careless at home? Too self-assured? Did he think that as his career prospered, all else would move ahead on a broad front, domestic life included? He was living out the myth of capitalist endeavour. There seemed no ripples on the surface.

She left just after her fortieth birthday. Her own life was at a watershed, in a state of flux. She had started up a part-time job, at his suggestion. The kids were getting older and were almost in their teens. He felt she needed more than just part-time badminton to keep her interests up, or so it looked to him from the perimeter fence.

Looking back now, he had noticed that 'She'd gone into a shell over the previous three months, had become much more remote, quiet and insular.' But he had missed reading the signs: 'What had happened is that she started her affair with the decorator.'

It was really unbearable for him. His reaction was to move out, withdraw from the scene of the crime, not allow it to find him out. 'I'll sell the house. I'm not even going to live here.' His beautiful home in London, his own house.

Withdrawal was his way of coming to terms with what was really happening. He calls it 'fair enough', a deliberate understatement. He buys her a car, gets her another house, puts their house on the market. The business analogy would be: the company has collapsed, sell the assets. But the blandness is deceptive. He is keeping the hurt at bay. His emotional life has caught up with him; it's been underused in his marriage.

As so often happens, the problems get displaced. Their daughter seems to be bearing the brunt. She is acting up at school, giving the teachers hell, dramatically expressing the furore that her parents could not express. Jung has a phrase about children living out the unlived life of the parents. Her disruption is getting worse, stopping teachers from getting on with their work, stopping things from coming together. A ghost in the machine, echoing her parents splitting. She is provoking anger all round her. She has been suspended and may be expelled from school – another divorce. Experts have been called in and confirm she is deeply hurt inside, her resentment at the break-up of her parents' marriage coming out as aggression against teachers at school who are figures of authority in *loco parentis*. The pent-up frustration is being expressed via her. But she sits tight in the presence of the educational psychologist who interviews them as a family. She will not, cannot open up in front of her parents.

The younger child has taken up the 'other' position. He is quiet, accepting, instead of acting out, he keeps things in. They all say he is 'coping better'.

Graham would like to get the divorce 'sorted out' as quickly as possible, deal with the problem in his characteristic way, get it over and done with. But his wife, inexplicably, will not agree. He has to wait. In eighteen months time (or after two years) the separation agreement becomes a divorce automatically. A long wait. Perhaps she is deliberately drawing it out, parallelling the long years of waiting she feels she endured. Better make sure of the financial side, though. Is she really retaliating, forcing him to keep her pace now? He wished he knew.

Revenge is in the air. A hint of aggression comes out when he consoles himself with 'her living standards have fallen, and will continue to fall very dramatically.' Let her find out what it is like. He is not going to shift his ground. For him, faced with this crisis in midlife, the answer is to batten down the hatches, go on with the same as before, only more so. Take firmer control, better charge. It has worked before, so it should work again.

Perhaps it is better not to know how deeply involved she is with the other person. Keep bad news at a distance. Kill Pheidippides. Perhaps she will come back, see the error of her ways.

'We never argued' he says. Was this collusion, part of a joint attempt to sustain the myth of a good marriage? A pact to avoid psychological pain, fearing rejection, anger and by the same token missing out on experiencing the longing, the wanting of each other.

'We never argued, never . . . you know . . . no problems like that.' It has meant missing out on development, on pain to survive from and confront, and then to start up anew.

'She didn't give the marriage a chance. She just said, "No that's it. Bang."' He'd have liked a second go, a second chance, to make it good again. But she just blew up, boiled over, 'after all these years'.

Still, there is no use crying over spilt milk. 'I'm resigned to it now – I don't look back – I really only look forward. I go out quite a lot. Disappointing and sad in a way, but then that's life I suppose.' Cover over the traces. Human kind cannot bear very much reality.

'I wouldn't go back now – no way – no way.' There's a lingering doubt in the repetition. Is he toying with the idea, wondering, speculating momentarily about the possibility? Does it repress a wish? Ah, if only . . .

'She says things to me like "You never understood me"' – an indictment that he can just about accept, as he never believed she was going to do what she eventually did. But there is brooding anger underneath. It gets displaced onto the children, particularly the daughter. 'They had all the good things in life, and I can't afford to give it to them any more.'

He's hardened himself up, become tougher. 'I do feel as though I'm quite hard now . . . I can be more calculating. It's part of my job, looking at things and being clinical, analytical and I tend to do that with relationships now.' Same mixture as before only more strongly so. Perhaps he's noticing himself more, letting these notions surface. Before he just took the attitudes home with him from the office and carried on.

He used to take relationships for granted, supposed they 'just happened' and didn't really worry about them 'too much'. The present upheaval came as a complete surprise. Relationships exist, they either work or they don't. The main aim is to provide a happy home, husband at work, wife at home, each consecrated in their roles. Static. Now he's baffled by his wife's present attitude, her 'acceptance' of the situation. She says things like 'Oh we were happily married for seventeen years, got nothing against marriage at all.' He can't follow this at all. He feels somehow she has usurped the whole institution of marriage and can't reconcile her walking out with what she's just said.

He takes his own aggression out on the football field and 'I go out and drink quite a bit.'

But for him too the collapse of his marriage has been some sort of release:

I feel more secure than I did in a family situation. I felt very much the responsibility of being a provider . . . I felt those responsibilities quite heavily. Now I don't have them and as a result, so my director tells me, in the last twelve to eighteen months I have worked better. It surprised me because I just do things now and if it goes wrong I say 'Tough'. Maybe it's a little bit arrogant but I'm reasonably secure in what I do to know that I'm not going to lose my job or anything like that. If I do something wrong I might get admonished for it, but it's not that important. I don't have anybody else to worry about really. My secretary and the people around me are saying I'm good fun.

He has found compensation for the collapse of his marriage in work where his self-esteem and career have been steadily ascending over the years.

David Armstrong, whom we first met in Chapter 3, went through a similar sequence of events when his first marriage collapsed:

I never believed my marriage would break up. I mean, I just did not believe it could happen. It was totally my fault. My wife was very, very sweet – very sweet. She was Pisces, I'm Scorpio and she's a real sweetie-pie, literally, but I mean I was working so bloody hard I was never home. I was so embroiled in business, I was thirty-one years old before I noticed a tree. I mean I could actually look at a park and not think anything other than 'What a crashing bore.' My friend, my close friend, actually said, 'You might be giving your wife everything but you're not giving her what she really wants.' I said, 'Well, what do you mean?' He said, 'All she wants is to be with you more.' I was working in a factory that was turning over twenty-four hours a day, I had to be there about 5.30 am and wouldn't be home until 7 pm or 8 pm and then might be called out a couple of times in the night. Certainly in the last twelve months we did little together and we had a young child, our daughter was only two and we did the classic trip. I mean, I can't believe it, looking back. But we actually did the classic trip of 'let's have a child to bring us closer together' and what in fact it did was keep me out of the door more. I didn't think it at the time, but now when I lecture I actually say 'Look, people that do consistent overtime, I must conclude, as a psychologist, they just don't want to go home' and I was the classic. It's almost like all the things that I'm telling people now – I know what it's like because I've done it. I'd fallen into exactly the same trap, you know.

6

Alone

Last night I dreamt of a jauntier principle of order
Today I eat my usual diet of shadows

THEODORE ROETHKE

Being on your own can be a mixed blessing. The first story is of an individual who has found himself unexpectedly on his own as a single-parent father. It has caused him to make major revisions in his working life and discover sides of himself that he didn't know were there. The interview took place while his crisis was still going on.

Bill Mason was in the outer office with a colleague. They are discussing uniforms and looked uncomfortable at desks, out of place. Bill is tall, wearing a blue 'operations' shirt. A leading fireman, he had only been on desk duty for two weeks, arranged by the service because of his personal difficulties. He went through an earlier crisis some years back at the break-up of his marriage when everything seemed to go wrong, his mother dying on holiday at the same time; now he's in another crisis having to adjust his working life to take care of his son, hence the desk job. The irony is that he's spent most of his life trying not to avoid being tied down, as his story shows. Fate or a combination of circumstances has brought him round from the devil-may-care attitude of youth to an acceptance of responsibility and of commitment. At forty-one he is prepared to make personal sacrifices for his son's future based on an enduring, realistic attitude 'Just carry on your life. Do what you can while you can.' He's not out of his crisis yet, but perhaps his willingness to confront it and tackle his problems will deliver a solution for him.

I'm normally a Leading Fireman, normally ride on fire engines. I enjoy it. I've been in the fire service seventeen years now, joined when I was twenty-four and I'll be forty-one this year. Never had any regrets at all about joining – if you're looking for an easy life, forget it. If you're looking for a contented family life, a regular settled family life, forget it.

Who, if they have young children, enjoys going to work on a Christmas Day shift or at four o'clock on a Sunday afternoon in the middle of summer, saying 'That's it, I'm off to work, bye-bye everybody'? It's hard to drag yourself away at times but you have to do it. But there again if you're not prepared to do that, you wouldn't be in the fire service. It's that type of job.

When I left school I worked for Whitbreads the brewers and they wanted me to train as a computer programmer. Whitbreads were going to install what at that time was one of the most up to date computer systems, it was an IBM 360. This was the mid-sixties when people's attitudes in the City to dress, to rules and regulations were such that if you did not conform you were out. It was very rigid and I just didn't enjoy it. I went off on holiday to Yugoslavia, spent a week out there camping, got involved with the first Yugoslavian Motor Cycle Grand Prix. We were staying at a camp site which one weekend was suddenly flooded by all these vans and trailers and it was the Grand Prix Motor Cycle set moving in. Not as flash and advanced and money-involved as now, because at that time it was enthusiasts with their clapped-out vans and all the bikes – all their money went on their bikes. I'd been unsettled anyway in the job and I decided there was more to life that sitting in an office with books of figures and tables and counting money every Thursday when the van delivered all the cash. I just wrote my resignation on the back of a post-card and sent it in.

But I took my time coming back from Yugoslavia and in the third week of August I went into the office to collect my bits and pieces and my manager said 'Well, where have you been?' I said 'Didn't you get my card?' He said, 'Well, we don't take notice of things like that.' I said 'Well I meant it.' He replied, 'Well hard luck, if you mean it, we want your notice now and you've got to work your notice' which I did. From there I packed up and bummed off again.

I applied to London Transport for a job and I became a guard on the District Line of the Underground and did that for three years and got sick and tired of that. The attitude from the general public was such that you were really looked down upon as scum. Terrible thing to say but people really did look down upon you. And I couldn't stick that, so I packed up in the May. Then I went bumming around again. Came back through the summer. At the end of the summer I went to British United Airways, as was, which later became part of British Caledonian. When the two airlines amalgamated it was a case of last in, first out.

Then I went to Sainsburys and they tried the same as London Transport had done. 'Your past work experience means that we would like you to train as assistant manager.' 'Thank you, not interested.' Again they couldn't understand my attitude. I just didn't want to know. I stayed there through the winter and then about February or March I applied to join the

Fire Brigade. I had a letter asking me to enrol – that was June 1971 and I went up and started my training After about a month I suppose, I was late for parade one morning along with another fellow in the squad, and it was really strict discipline. The following morning we were out on what we call 'punishment detail'. Full fire gear – and there were others for dirty shoes, or being incorrectly dressed, because they'd been out for various reasons.

There were eight or ten of us on this punishment detail. The other squads were doing their square bashing and we went round in full fire gear to a playground adjacent to the training centre. It was just an open play space, and we were marched round the street by an instructor, you don't just wander round the street. We were marched round and our punishment was to run around this area in full fire gear until we were told to stop and we just kept going and going and going. This other chap and I, who had been late the previous day, we just kept going but we were leaning on each other for support. All the others gradually dropped out but to give him his due the instructor kept going, he wasn't just there to instruct; he was fitter than all of us and he kept going with us, but after that we went back and we were told 'Right get yourselves ready for your first lesson.' Unfortunately for me it was a drill session and we always started off our drill session with a carry-down where you go up a ladder – we don't have them now – it's a 45-ft ladder on a carriage with large wheels for manoeuvring it. We pitched it to the third floor and the whole squad ran up, and you just picked one of the chaps up and carried him down it. Unfortunately we had a chap in our squad who was 15 stone. He was a little bit nervous of heights and he tended to tense up a bit when he was being carried, so everyone else tried to avoid picking him up, and he was the one I was left with. I said 'Right, come on Smudger, we've got to go' and I picked him up and I got out on the ladder and I'd gone down about three rounds when I realized that I was far weaker than I felt. Suddenly, having come down about three rounds, I couldn't put him back into the building because I was below the sill level. I felt my left leg slip and just went through. He was on a safety harness. Unfortunately I wasn't on anything and I slipped and came down, broke my nose, split my head and landed on the metal frame at the bottom of the ladder. Landed on that, on my back laying across it; head down one side, feet the other, bloody and a bit of a mess. I got up and walked away and was taken off to hospital. There, I was patched up and taken home. I'm not sure if it was the following day or the day after – I think I had one day at home – and the day after that I turned up at work because I felt that if I didn't go in I'd sit at home and perhaps never go back at all. So I went back and they took one look at me and said 'No, there's no way you can carry on.' I said 'Course there is, I can attend the lectures, do the paperwork; I can stand out in the yard doing questions and answers with the other fellers. Maybe I can't run about. I can't climb ladders. I appreciate that. You won't let me but I can deal with the rest of it.' They agreed and said 'Ok, we'll let you carry on providing the hospital says so.' So I went up to the hospital, saw the doctor, came back with my note from the doctor and carried on.

Fortunately for me, as soon as the doctors passed me fit for carrying on full duties, my instructors and the other fellows in the squad gave up their tea breaks and lunch breaks, so that I could have extra drill on the practical side, that I hadn't been able to do, and I managed to pass. I don't know how, because my chest felt as if it was like an oven. All my breath, everything was red raw. Simply because I got so fit. I'd done nothing and then was trying to get fit again with all the running around, but thanks to all the help that I got from the instructors and the other fellers in the squad, I managed to pass out, and I was posted to my first station. And I always remember, when I got that posting, you're all sitting down and the instructor comes in and reads out the name and where you're posted to, and a number of fellows said to me – and they weren't recruits, they were instructors and qualified firemen that were up on other courses to further their career – and they all said to me 'How the bloody hell did you get that station?' because at that time it was a station that lots of people wanted to get to, but you couldn't because it was very much a closed shop. It was sort of dead man's shoes so to speak. No one wanted to leave. And for some reason I was posted there and I stayed there until I was promoted in March 1982 and, I don't know, but if I hadn't been promoted then, it's quite likely I would still be there now.

Promotion was not something that I had gone out looking for. I'm not one of those people that sits down and thinks 'I want this, I want promotion, I'm going to go for it.' But I knew that I was becoming stale there. I'd been there for so long. I jokingly say to people 'They promoted me to get rid of me.' I was becoming like part of the furniture. I got a new posting because I got married in 1978 and I was living in a flat with the wife and two little boys just at the top of Brixton Hill. We lived there through the time of the riots, and I became more and more depressed. Some of the people that lived around us were very nice; some of them were animals, black or white. Couple living next door to us, West Indian couple, I would have done anything for them and they would have done anything for us. Other people in the block, well, you didn't dare turn your back on. Didn't dare leave your washing out. You know, it was that sort of an area. I became depressed.

Anyway, we managed to get out. We also had my wife's children from a previous marriage living with us. We were living in a two-bedroomed flat and we got out and bought a house in West London and we seemed to be going along Ok. I had a bit of an upset with my wife's son from the previous marriage. He went through a spell when he just wasn't trying at school amongst other things, and I knew darn well he could do a lot better, because we were getting reports back from school about his work, and he was doing far harder work at home in the homework that we were setting for him. He just sort of stopped trying – whether he was at a time when he started resented me as he wanted to be with his natural father, I don't know.

He went back to France eventually to his grand-parents and stayed there. My wife was very upset. It came out during the divorce, during one of the arguments, that she felt that I had driven her son away and she hadn't loved me since then. It's one of those things isn't it?

When I was promoted in the March to West London, I was very apprehensive, because having spent eleven years almost in the one area, you get to know all the watches, and all the blokes and this was like going to another brigade. It was across the river; you didn't really know what to expect, especially having the responsibility of a rank as well now. And quite honestly I couldn't have fallen in with a better bunch of blokes. Over the years I've had about four offers to come back over this side – fellows that were retiring 'Do you want to come back over this side – I'm retiring, it doesn't matter to me – do a mutual exchange, you can come back over here; I'm going to be pensioned off so it doesn't matter.' I said 'No thanks, I'm happy where I am because I've got a bunch of blokes there I know I can trust. I don't have to tell them what to do. It doesn't matter what the situation is, they work on their own initiative without orders, but they work as a team, and it's great, it really is great.' I was very happy.

The marriage sort of ticked along; we were buying this house, but it's like so many things, when you buy your first home. Money always seems to be in short supply. We only had the furniture that we'd brought from the two-bedroomed flat. While we were living in the flat we bought new beds and a new three-piece. We bought new carpets when we moved into the house, but with four kids (at the time the youngest was two) it's pretty hard. Anyway, as you do, you make do and you work on. I was looking for other ways of ekeing out the money. I took on an allotment and I took on a second one. We had two dogs and as I say, just having the single salary just didn't seem to be working, so things were a struggle and we couldn't decorate as often as we liked. We couldn't buy the new furniture. We couldn't go out because we didn't have the money (we were saving for something in the home you know). It was one of those situations, but we carried on. The kids seemed happy enough; we took them out whenever we could, even if it was only down to the river fishing. And they seemed quite happy.

Then we had a retirement do. One of the fellows was going to retire. My wife knew it was coming up. All the wives were invited obviously and she said 'Yes' she would go. And I came in about 4 o'clock on the afternoon that we were going to go to this retirement do. And I took the dogs out for a good run. My step-daughter was at work, but she was going to look after the boys. When I came back with the dogs, I ran a bath, had a cup of tea. Been in the bath, came down, was sitting down in the front room with the boys. I heard the front door close and I called out 'Is that you?' No answer. And I looked out and I saw it was my wife walking out the door. She'd said when I brought the dogs back that she didn't really want to go because it would end up like most fire brigade 'dos'. All the blokes standing in the corner, getting drunk, laughing, joking, telling stories about previous fires etc., and all the women sitting in a corner. I said 'Well, you've had the invitation, you've been invited, all the wives are going to be there; if you don't want to go it's up to you.' But I saw her go out and the step-daughter wasn't home yet so I said to the boys 'That's good isn't it, mum's gone out, she knows we were going out to a retirement do.' The boys turned round and said quite unthinkingly 'Don't worry dad, Jeanie will look after us, she always looks after us when mum goes out and you're on nights.' So that was the first I knew my wife was having an affair.

Needless to say, I didn't go to the retirement do that night. I phoned up with my apologies. I lied, told them that the wife was ill, and stayed at home. Sent the kids off to bed and sat there. My guts were going round and there were all sorts of thoughts going through my brain. I sat there watching a film with Jeanie and I got fed up with it and I just couldn't concentrate. I said to Jeanie 'Sorry Jeanie, I'm going to bed.' This was 11.30. I said 'Your mum's still out, don't know if she's got her keys' and I just went to bed but I couldn't sleep, sitting there, tossing and turning, sitting up looking out the window. And 2.50 in the morning I heard a clip-clop, clip-clop, and she came up the path. I'd gone down at 1 o'clock and bolted all the doors, and she came to the side and tried the back door. She came over the side gate, tried the back door and couldn't get in and then she got a set of steps out and a long pole and she was tapping on the daughter's bedroom window, and when I heard that I went downstairs to open the back door and said a few choice words to her. Asked her what the bloody hell she thought she was up to; what time do you think this is, etc.; why do you bother coming home at this time of the morning – you know, nasty things, but I'd sat there and stewed for so long I just couldn't help it. They're not the sort of things I normally say, not even to blokes. But anyway, because of this, other things that had happened previously started coming back to me and I started putting two and two together. When I came home from work on the Saturday, they work Saturdays, she wasn't at home.

There was a letter waiting for me, and she came in about 10 o'clock that evening. Kids were in bed and I tried sitting there talking to her and I couldn't. The following night when I came home I still couldn't talk to her. On the Monday the kids were at school and we sat down and we had a talk. I told her exactly how I felt, and told her that she had to make up her mind. Whether she wanted him or me. What she wanted to do. I didn't put a time limit on it, just said 'You've got to make up your mind; I can't live like this; I want to know what's going on' because all I'd done had been for her and the kids to the extent that that evening coming to work I'd given her the last penny out of my pocket. Well, it became a standing joke about the way I used to dress, always riding a pushbike, and yes, I was upset. And I told her I just couldn't go on like it. I wanted to know what was going on, you know, to make up her mind. So she told me, this was in the November, and she eventually made up her mind and in the March I filed for divorce. I say 'eventually made up her mind' but even had she said 'no' she didn't want him, I think by that time it would have been too late.

So we agreed what we were going to do: sell the house. The two boys used to argue. The elder boy, Billy, was very much a mother's boy, whereas the younger one, Andrew, was a dad's boy. And they did argue, and it wasn't just sort of brotherly arguing, it was as if they were taking sides and fighting out the battle for us, so we decided that we would take one boy each. She would have the younger boy, Andrew, to stay with her when I was working weekends and when I was free at weekends and during the holidays the other boy, Billy, would stay with me. We would sell the house and the solicitor had told me that I could stay there with the boy if I so desired, but during this time my mother died. She'd had open heart surgery. My parents had gone on holiday. This was at the time I'd actually filed for divorce. They'd gone on holiday and my mother had died whilst my parents were on holiday. My father had been in bad health for about eight years and had retired early because of it. He had gone progressively downhill healthwise since mum died. Then this proposal was put forward to the court for the care of the children: she was going to set up home with her boyfriend and look after Billy. I was going to live close to my parents, initially moving in with them until I found a flat close by. They would look after Andrew while I was at work and get him off to school, but the rest of the time he would be with me. But as I say, in the meantime my mother had died and my father's health had gone downhill. He wouldn't come and live in the house even though I thought 'Right I've got the house straight and even have central heating which is good for his health.' He wouldn't come over, he wouldn't even come over to visit me in the house, so we sold the house and I moved in with Andrew to my father's house last February. Since then my father's health got worse, in fact he died a month ago yesterday.

But that's why I'm on day work now. We divorced. My wife and I agreed what we were going to do. The house was sold. Paid off the mortgage, split what was left between us. There's no hate. I mean, I'm taking my boy over there this week-end. We're going over tonight, I will go over there, take him over. He rings his mum from the station and then we meet them walking down the road. My older boy comes with her, so that I see Billy and he'll spend the weekend with her and I go and collect him again on Sunday evening. Similarly last weekend, on Friday, I collected Billy after school – he stayed with me for the weekend and I took him back. There's no hate between us, there never has been quite honestly. I loved her too much for that and couldn't hate her despite what happened. Couldn't live with her again though, as much as I love her. Couldn't live with her again. I think it hasn't helped me for any future relationships.

As far as I'm concerned now, my boys are my life and that's it. As far as the job's concerned, I still love it. I didn't have any problems when my father used to look after my son whilst I was on nights, but now I haven't got anybody else. I have a sister but she lives down in the West Country, so I have no one else up here who could look after the boy for me. I've been given a three month temporary posting on day work here to enable me to look after my boy, and hopefully get something sorted out, because in the mean time the house that I'm living in, which is my father's is a rented house. It's a council property. My parents had lived there for twenty-two years but they were never in a position to buy it. My father and I were going to buy it but there's a clause that I would have to live in the property for twelve months with my father before we could apply to buy it. In point of fact when my father died, I'd lived in the house for one year and ten days, so I qualified on the time scale, but obviously in that time there's absolutely no way that papers and house purchase could go through, so that's it. I'm in a position now where I'm on day work which I don't really want, so that I can look after my boy and sort out my domestic situation. There is nothing I would like more than to go back onto shift work, but I can't honestly see it happening because I have no one to look after my boy, and that has got to be my priority. The end of my marriage – as I say the love I had for my wife and the way it all ended – soured me for any sort of relationship, I think. Certainly at the present time, anyway. Maybe in a few years time, I don't know, my attitude may change. I don't honestly know.

That's the position I'm in at the moment. After all these years – it is now twenty-one years since I left the city – I now find myself sitting in an office working nine till five which I strove to get rid of all those years ago. Almost back to square one. I don't own a property anymore. I'm living in rented accommodation at the moment. I've got this feeling that perhaps for the next ten years or so I might well have to be stuck in an office.

My boy now, he was nine in January, he's a very good kid, he really is. I'm getting signals now from my elder boy that he's unhappy and he wants to come over 'now grandad's not there' and look after Andrew and live with us. I think he's going through the phase that my wife's son from her previous marriage was going through when I had problems with him. Seeing Billy and the way he's feeling, I'm now beginning to realize what the other boy was going through when I was having problems. Everything's up in the air, and I'm just taking things day by day.

I was very fortunate really because the fellows that I worked with at the fire station have seen me go through a happily married stage and they've seen me go through the divorce. They've known the situation with my father's ill-health. In fact I had the phone call: I was on duty and we were out at a fête when the phone call came through to say that my mother had been taken to hospital while they were on holiday, so the fellows at work have gone through all of this with me as well and supported me, and I was actually off sick at the time my father died and my station officer phoned me at home and said 'Look, you've been off sick just over a week now, how are you coping, how's your father, do you want some help?' and I said 'Don't worry about dad anymore, dad died last night.' He said 'Right, do you want anyone over there now, do you want any help, do you want anything done?' and I said 'No thank you.' But he came back to me within two hours and said 'Do you want to go onto day work, fire prevention to tide you over and help you look after your boy until things are sorted out? If you do, say "yes" and it's yours.' I said 'Yes please.' I couldn't say anything else because it took so many worries off my shoulders immediately: concern about the job and looking after Andrew. Until I got my motorbike I travelled on public transport, which was two hours plus each way each day.

The quicker I can get this lot sorted out, the better. You tend to come home from work, go indoors and do whatever is necessary. As I say, my marriage has soured me for any sort of relationship. I don't know. Once I know what's happening with the house, I've got to decide where I'm going to live. If they say 'No, there is no tenancy' then I've got to think seriously about where I'm going to live.

As I mentioned earlier, the other alternative is perhaps to move down to the West Country where my sister has offered to look after Andrew for me. But my chances of getting a job down there are just about nil because county brigades take the viewpoint 'Well, if we have a vacancy, we will take a local man who perhaps hasn't got a job at all.' That's a viewpoint I can understand. Another option is to move down there, for my four days off and come up here for my two day shifts. As soon as my second day shift has finished I could go back down there so that I've got the night and the day there and then come up here for my night duties. But I don't know, I'm not bothered by the travelling but it's being away from the boy. The imposition – because it is an imposition on my sister – worries me. Although she said 'Yes' she would look after him, to look after someone while you're working locally for a night shift is one thing, but to look after someone, even though he is your nephew for two days at a time – I don't know. It's something that I've thought about but we haven't actually discussed.

It means I'm moving further and further away from Billy at a time when I feel he needs me. He needs to be able to see me and contact me. I don't know. I really really don't know. I'm in a mess, quite honestly. At the moment I've got so many things to do, I don't seem to have enough hours in the day. I mean, Andrew goes to bed, then I start washing up, because you can't just go home from here. Alright, you prepare a meal the night before, you put it in the oven, you set the timer and it will be cooking, and then you've got to spend your time with the boy. You can't say 'Sorry I'm busy I'm cooking the meal' or 'No I'm doing the washing'. You've got to spend your time with the boy and he goes up to bed to 8.30. Until then we have our meal, he sits and reads to me, or I read. I read to him at bedtime because it's something I've always done with all the kids; we'll play a game; or do whatever he wants to do, basically. Sometimes I let him have his radio on or cassette or something or sit in bed and read comics, but its definitely lights out at 9 and its usually 8.30 in bed and no lights, but occasionally I relent. He looks upon it as a treat then. If he gets it every night, it's not the same, is it?

Once he's in bed, then I start doing the washing up or whatever needs doing. But a number of times I've done the washing up and sat down with a cup of tea and that's it, I've fallen asleep only to wake up maybe half an hour later. It gets you like that, but what the heck? It's the boy's life. I say, if it means I've got to stay on days, alright, I'll stay on days. It's something you've got to put up with isn't it. You can't penalize your kids. I get one day off a fortnight, so I tend to do the washing either when he's at school or when he's in bed. Because you do it one night, it dries overnight, when he's gone to bed the second night, you're doing your ironing. It's got to be fitted in with him so that the boy's not neglected. At the weekends when Billy has been over to me, I've managed to do the shopping during the week in my lunch hour or on the way home, so that when I've got the boys there and we go out, I've got all the time for them. We can go out and it's not a case of 'Oh well I've got to get some potatoes and some bread and milk, or got to do this or . . .' No, the housework and everything else goes by the board while I've got them for the weekend.

Well in many ways I still think of myself as younger, despite suddenly seeing the boys grow up into the size that they are. The father/son relationship nowadays isn't the same as it was with my father and myself. I look upon them as friends as much as sons, and hopefully they look upon me in the same way. I think because of what we tend to do silly things together which my father and I would never have dreamed of doing.

I was not as close to my father as I feel that my boys are to me. Yes, there was a love and respect there, but I couldn't go up to him, as my boys do, throw my arms round him and kiss him and mess about with him. There was a love and respect there but, as I say, not the way there is between my boys and myself. Whether that is because people's attitudes are changing – bearing in mind the early fifties when children were seen and not heard and had to be very respectful. Some people let their children go far too far nowadays and crawl all over them, but my boys know when to stop. If they don't they know what to expect. They know how far they can push me. We lay down certain guidelines . . . 'guide-lines' – that sounds rather severe – but good manners and good be-haviour. They know what they can do and what they can't. And that's not only with me but with other people too; they know not to butt in on conversations and go on which is really common decency, but so many children seem to be lacking it nowadays. They know how to twist me round their finger, know how to get things out of dad, as all kids do. But nowadays parents have the money to be able to give these things to their kids.

There is no doubt about the strength of the relationship between father and son. For all its trials and tribulations, it has sustained him and given him a sense of purpose in his post-divorce period. Necessity has revealed to him the hidden strengths of the family bond. It's been some sort of lesson to him, helping him shift from his avowed independence of earlier years to a recognition of the value and resourcefulness to be found in others. But he's still a firefighter by nature, rather than a Prevention Officer.

I've never actually gone looking for problems. I've waited for them to rear their ugly head and then looked for a solution. I've never been a person to ask for help. I've always been independent in that way. I'd rather struggle with something than ask someone to help me. Simply because I don't want to be beholden to anybody. I don't know, perhaps it's a silly attitude. Perhaps that's not even right, no, it's not really being beholden. I will help other people if I can, I'll do anything, but I personally wouldn't go and ask anyone else for help. If someone offers then I will accept gratefully because they've offered, but I wouldn't go and ask. Maybe that's a silly attitude I don't know, but that's me. It's the way I've always been and I can't see me changing. I'm one of these people that tend to face things when they're there, right in front of me. Otherwise, just carry on your life. Do what you can while you can. And when there is a problem and you can't dodge it, Ok you've got to face up to it and then you do the rest. But I'm not the sort to try to find ways round a problem for months before, when there is no real problem. Some people spend their lives planning, don't they? And then something happens and all their plans go out the window.

He agreed however that speaking at such length and with such frankness during this interview had helped him 'get things off his chest' and that this may have been the reason why he 'subconsciously' agreed to talk. It is part of his gradual shift in position to taking on a wider sense of responsibility. You get the feeling he is learning as he goes along, and is willing to do so.

This next story also focuses on an interim phase in life, but here the echoes are of displacement and security, finding a home and being an outsider, uprooting, settling down and being on one's own again. Louis Kaye was born in Poland in 1935, his family as Jews being forced to flee hurriedly with no possessions at the outbreak of war in 1939. His father, mother, himself and a cousin, who happened to be staying with them, got on the last train out of Warsaw to Roumania whence they crossed Europe on a closed train to the English Channel and then to London, where he has lived ever since. Those early experiences are indelibly marked on his memory and form a sort of *leitmotif* to his life. Now at midlife he faces questions about future directions to take, as he is living on his own again, with two marriages behind him.

He looks on his present stage of life as 'an interim phase, having to juggle with all sorts of possibilities, of keeping myself open, nor too set in my ways. I don't want to prevent the possibility of a relationship of any consequence developing, but, just in case it doesn't happen, I've got to be able to manage on my own.'

His unsettled start in life contributed to a feeling of insecurity.

As far back as I can remember, even as far back as the age of seven, I've had a conscious awareness that life is very limited. When I was in my twenties without a clear idea of what I wanted to do, I was pulled in a number of different directions, mainly because none of the career paths recommended themselves to me. I went to Oxford University and then did some research on memory for the Medical Research Council. My interest in the past and the way large social groups worked then took me to the Tavistock Clinic. There I 'discovered' psychoanalysis, excited by the prospect of at last finding a language that fitted the things I'd been talking and thinking about for so long, plus a group of people who thought the same way.

Psychoanalysis was a way of examining his own family history, principally the personality of his mother which he'd found so baffling: 'I couldn't understand why she did what she did. My mother was incomprehensibly out of touch in her response to me, for instance, if I asked her why something happened, she would classify that as being rude. I just could not get my mind round this.' He had always been closer to his father, a very warm man, whom he'd 'turn to not just for warmth and sympathy but for rational discussion'. He was 'a great source of strength, but when I was eleven he did me no service at all in going off to be a newspaper correspondent in Warsaw for four years, with only short periods of leave back in the UK'.

At the Tavistock he trained as a psychoanalyst, welcoming its ability to 'mitigate my depression and lead me to question assumptions more,' but, after a while, he decided he wasn't cut out to be a psychoanalyst. He was at a crossroads in his life, unsure what career to head for, uncertain about the future of his marriage. He had grown up admiring people such as Schweitzer for the way he had mapped out a clear plan for his life, deciding he was going to spend the first thirty years of his life organ-building and the next thirty years in medicine. But without such a programme himself, events tended to take charge, so that when in his mid-thirties he found himself without a career and his marriage in difficulties, he just stumbled through it. He didn't have a consciousness of 'this being it'. 'I didn't say to myself "Hang on, this is my midlife crisis." I just went through it.'

Louis Kaye was married shortly after leaving Oxford to a fellow student. Ten years later, he started to find himself 'increasingly uninvolved with my wife, we just didn't coincide any longer, it wasn't vicious or nasty. I didn't run her down; it got to the point where I just felt the situation was increasingly phoney.' In retrospect he thinks he had possibly gone into marriage in search of a 'sister or the sibling I never had' and he was happy to play 'the outcast, the depressed person – creative but difficult.' Marriage had been important in providing him with a family, security and stability, which he had missed out on earlier. He was an only child and most of his family had been killed in the Holocaust.

Yet here he was again backing out, leaving himself cast up without a family home or a career. The refrain of upheaval in his life was repeating itself. After his marriage broke up another relationship started, but it was volatile, unsettled and put him through what he terms as six years of 'pretty high temperature turbulence'. It was a 'really grim period, intense pain week after week, not knowing what the hell to do, whichever way I faced was intolerable'. It was a prolonged midlife crisis. He went into analysis again, helped by the generosity of some friends. Without this he would have collapsed, he now feels. He tried a second marriage that did not last.

Now he is on his own, faced with the major issue of 'What sort of personal life do I want? On my own or sharing? What sort of person would it be sensible for me to associate with?'

My constructive feeling at the moment is that I need to sit quietly for a while. Life is too unpredictable and relationships are always problematic. The answer is to leave them open, and that means leaving myself open as well. In many respects it's infinitely simpler being on one's own, not having to say 'That's lovely' when you didn't think it was lovely, or being able to hang something from the ceiling without having to consult someone else. Simple things, maybe, but also not so simple. It's quite seductive living on one's own but the disadvantages are an increased sense of isolation, with parents dying [his father died in 1974] or becoming senile as my mother has, and old friends moving away. When I talk to people twenty years older than me they confirm this perspective of the world becoming a progressively lonelier place. It's quite worrying.

As his present work involves quite a lot of travel, it cuts into his social life. 'Friends ring up and invite me out and I have to say I'll be away. They soon start thinking, "It's no point ringing him as he's bound to be away." I miss that enormously as my friends mean a great deal to me.' He sees a possible solution being 'a sort of sailor's marriage' – the advantage being, at his age, that a partner 'is likely to have her own career and interests, and each of us can get on with his or her own life'.

As in the previous story he's found the relationship with his own children of great help in this phase of his life. He's always enjoyed being a parent 'It's the Boy Scout part of me that likes leading the patrol into whatever lies ahead. I still enjoy that very much. That's consistently been a good department of life. I've never felt distanced from my kids.' In the last four or five years, he's had a lot more to do with them, and has much better relationships with each of them. The eldest comes round for dinner, to have a chat and talk about family friends and they can look back together at the years of marriage in a relaxed way. He finds it very supportive and strengthening. Last summer he took them all to a villa in the Mediterranean. The youngest came back and reported 'Dad's changed', echoing Mark Twain's remark that at sixteen he was appalled how insensitive and uncaring his parents were, while at twenty-one he was amazed how much they had changed.

But the central theme in much of his life has been to establish a secure sense of home.

A lot of my energy at the moment goes into playing around with these houses [he's just bought a large house in London, and has a cottage in Norfolk]. It's partly *per se* but it's also a creative outlet. I'm not interested in prettification, but in doing up houses that I can shape as home. Recently I was talking with some friends who included someone who'd come over from Germany just before the war and is half-Jewish herself. We were discussing the significance of home. Where is home? What is it those of us who've been displaced are looking for? I think about it a fair bit. I came to the conclusion it's the Baden Powell: home is you, you carry it around with you. It's something I rely on very much, the ability to make a home wherever I am. It's essentially a state of mind that will triumph over whatever physical drawbacks there are. A friend came here not so long ago and commented on the number of places you can put your feet up – a chaise longue and a sofa whose arm drops down. I hadn't consciously noticed this before but she's right. I seem to need to put my feet up, it's something quite basic and animal-like, the feeling of having a lair, pulling the leaves over your head for the winter. The word 'cosy', or its equivalent, is very important in my psychic life. I have to be sure to always organize things so that there will be an apple to eat and a cushion to sit on. It's obviously got something to do with being uprooted from Poland at a very young age, but it also goes much earlier than that. There's a story of me when I first started talking at the age of two, sitting by my cot and saying the Polish word for 'comfy' over and again.

So much displacement in his life has highlighted this question of belonging. Being Jewish he feels this strongly.

Anybody who lives in a society that's not their society, and every Jew is in that position outside of Israel, finds it a strain, there's no two ways about it. It's not easy to describe it. You're certainly always aware you're on the outside of things. I admit I've had a very easy and privileged life, never been hungry, never been challenged with loss of life at the point of a gun, never been in mortal danger and always had interesting things to do. I'm very grateful for that. But even so I still feel an outsider.

His life alternates between periods of attachment and non-attachment. Midlife, which he senses as a crucial phase, has brought this out into the open for him. He likes to keep a door open to allow memories to come back of that closed train across Europe. Once a survivor, always a survivor.
  The need to both keep options open and explore possibilities comes out again in the next story. Peter Newton is a builder in his early forties with a robust attitude to life. He has been through a stormy marriage, and is recently divorced. He is something of a wanderer: 'I never felt I had a home to go to until I got this place two to three years ago' and a deferrer, now torn between the wish to be on his own or to have a girl friend 'in tow'.

What I often feel is that these life crises that we lurch to are frequently little more than that. So that a fellow arrives at the age of forty, bored with his wife, irritated with the kids, sick to death of his job which he's been plodding away at for maybe twenty years or something, and his ego is getting dented on all sides – physically and emotionally. By emotionally I mean in the sense that just as he's bored with his wife, she's no longer buttering him up and telling him what a lovely fellow he is. She's saying 'You silly bum, get out of the way or do this or do that.' He's now a fixture, he's probably at the end of his particular road, of his career, so that suddenly a lot of the little dreams which had been there when he was in his early twenties about actually owning a BMW and a yacht and another house, are all beginning to fall through.

As for me, I'm still resolving all sorts of conflicts from my youth really, which is quite enough to keep me going without getting into the glooms of midlife depression. Actually my life, certainly over the last two to three years or so, if anything is getting better. On the whole, I've started to enjoy life. Can I say *more*, as each year goes by? That isn't to say there isn't plenty of grind of irritation and problems but what I feel about myself is that for numerous reasons it's really taken me up until now to grow up, or nearly grow up – I haven't anywhere near finished. I think things have got better around forty, that's when things tend to pick up.

Relationships for him are still unsettled.

Yes, that's right, I drive girl friends mad by not needing them enough. You can't have everything in life. I get near to the point of feeling emotionally exhausted, it's a problem a lot of people probably face. It's a curious area: on the one hand you want to indulge in all those things that mean something to you, your books, your music, your carpets, your fires, your woodwork and pictures; you want even sit quietly doing your own thing, eating your food when you want to eat it – wonderful feeling as long as the money is there. You can do what the hell you like, you know, get on a plane to Paris tonight and there's absolutely nothing to stop you, if there's money in the bank. But then, on the other hand, suddenly there's this other funny thing: what the hell's the point in going to Paris all by yourself? Why go to Paris surrounded by a bunch of strangers on a plane, to stay in a little hotel room that you don't know, and so on.

It's like a see-saw, with you on each end of it. On the one hand there's emotional warmth plus obviously sexual outlets and things like that and on the other hand there is a conflict between men and women that I can't be dogmatic about because I'm continually puzzled, amused and very uncertain with women. I mean, I was with somebody that I don't have any relation with and we both know there's not likely to be one for all sorts of reasons, so I can only think she feels very free to talk to me. She hasn't got evil little guards and precautions, she's a capable, very good-looking woman of fifty and leads a fine social life. Very active and so on and she said 'God, Peter, I want a fortnightly man. Why can't I find a fortnightly man?' and I'm sure there are an awful lot of women who are like that. But hang me, get them to admit that to some fellow who is either slightly interested in them or who they feel interested in, and it's very hard to do it. Somehow a certain cloying emotion, that's an unfortunate word but it's cloying if you're on the wrong side of it, gets in the way.

It gives him cause to reflect on the sort of entanglements he habitually gets himself into.

Suddenly you find you're in a relationship and all this damned business starts up again. 'Well, why can't I see you on Saturday Peter?' and 'You know Saturday's the only day I'm really free.' 'This has cropped up, shall we go down and see my parents?' or 'So and so's having a party.' The next thing you know it's Wednesday night, and then Saturday and it's 10 o'clock Sunday morning and I want to get back here and spend a couple of hours reading the divine words of Thomas Carlyle for God's sake and she says 'What are you going now for – already?' She would want me padding round the damned living room or taking her goddamned dog for a walk or going for a stroll in the park, and that's all very nice but I'm afraid if I have a choice between two hours of Thomas Carlyle and that, it's no contest.

I mean, I'm a softie by nature. I don't like grief, I've seen too much of it, both in my mother when I was being raised and then in my marriage, the whole bit. And I do object to the fact that nowadays the only way to achieve some positive things in life is often being rather unkind to people or being very self-sacrificing. You could easily just come to the conclusion 'Right, sod it, I'm going to be bloody celibate and I'm not interested in any emotional relationships' and that's it and if some nice little dolly-bird happens to drape herself round me at a party on a Saturday night, then whoopee, but by Sunday morning 'Forget all about it baby.' You get involved in that sort of life and you're in great danger then of finding yourself drawn into cruddy parties on Saturday night on an off-shot of the bloody dolly-bird. Who wants to do that when you're forty, even assuming that you're going to be successful anyway, which is a big *if*, but assuming you are? So, that is a dilemma which is not an easy one to resolve, I must confess, and I think it is because there is a distinct gulf there between the male and the female. The male can be much more dispassionate, which is not to say he's uncaring, but he can be more objective about his emotional life. He can treat it as a much more 'matter of fact' business, it's as important to him but not with the same all pervading obsessiveness, maybe that's a bit unkind, not with the same intensity that I sense women have.

Looking ahead, he considers his future.

I'd be very content with one mate. In fact, yes, definitely. I'd want that because even more important, even if it's only fortnightly, is when one does go to bed at night and you think, not even in a sexual way, you just think it would be nice to have another body there, warm and cosy and bumpy and soft – lovely. But I suppose I can live without it. It's a price to pay but everything's got a price, there's no free lunches.

I have a dream. Certainly as far as my work is concerned, age and infirmity will start to put limitations on the work I can do. There will come a point when I'm simply physically not up to it. I mean when I think about

getting into my fifties climbing up a triple extension bloody ladder on a
freezing cold winter's day, fixing the bloody roofs or whatever or crawling
around on the floorboards and loft spaces and all this nonsense and
humping bricks around, there would certainly be a point where you think
'Right, quite enough of that.' What I would really love to do, quite
frankly, is to be a writer, and there's nothing new about that. That my
marriage interrupted. I have just, literally just, started. I mean, I felt I
had an awful lot of reading to do before I could confidently begin.
Anybody can sit there and just let all sorts of stuff come out. I am a great
believer in the craft of writing as a real craft, but I tend to have a very bird
brain. You know, it does flit around a lot – it goes off on all sorts of strange
tangents and makes connections all over the shop.

What lies ahead for him is full of appealing uncertainty.

Up to the age of twenty, a young man only thinks about sex, and after
twenty and up to thirty all he thinks about is money, between thirty and
forty all he thinks about is power. After that he says he's not quite sure
what he thinks about!

**Both the previous stories are of people who have come out of marriage
and are now on their own. The next story is of someone who has chosen to be
on his own, as it seems to befit his temperament. Victor Trumper is a
traveller through life, engaging and disengaging himself from relationships
and commitments. At heart he's a romantic, life for him is full of bright
starts. As the interview shows, he's still shackled to some extent by his
upbringing, with its mixture of advantage and entrapment. He's lived out
this paradox for some years. Now at forty-seven, still not married, his
anxieties about time running out are beginning to break through. He's used
to living on a knife edge ('I carry things to the edge of disaster') and, while
his optimism seems to replenish itself ('Something will turn up') his fears
that he is heading for disaster increase.**

Part of my midlife crisis is that I hardly ever go to my place of work [a
specialist bookshop he owns] which I am utterly bored with but can't
think what to do next. If I give it up then I've got absolutely nothing. I find
it impossible to find any sort of interest in it. I sit here in a terrible muddle,
broker and broker and broker. I'd willingly change my life, if I knew what
I wanted to do. Then I'd be ruthless about doing it.

I've had the bookshop practically all my life, endless stops and starts
and leaving for other things and then coming back. I entered it by mistake
and I've more or less stuck with it ever since. I don't feel it's me even
though I've done it for twenty-five years. I intended to do something
completely different which I had to put off, and I've sort of stuck with it.

Originally I'd planned to go to film school but then I got ill. I re-applied to the film school but if I'd re-applied with more vigour I'd have got in. Maybe deep down I was frightened. I can remember being that, but I'm just terribly lazy and it's mucked up many things.

Victor's start in life seemed privileged. He went to Eton and then on to Cambridge to read History.

I got fed up with it at the end, but I enjoyed it too. By the end I wanted to get out, I spent more time in London than Cambridge. I was much younger than everybody else, practically everybody else had been in National Service. I felt terrible, everybody else had seen the world and I had been solidly, efficiently educated for thirteen years without a break. Enough is enough. I came to an agreement with the tutor that I wasn't going to do any work and we drank in the pub once a week, it seemed agreeable to him.

Bookselling suited him to begin with.

I was actually very good at it and I did feel enthusiastic for some years. It's damned difficult to make money out of selling books, but I did. I wouldn't be living here if I hadn't made money out of it and I'm now rapidly losing, or I've lost, the money that I made out of it. It's taken exactly the same amount of time to reduce myself to where I was before I started. I have a fantastically good memory, which is really all it is about. I mean, I can remember seeing a book fifteen years ago and I know exactly what it should have and why it's important. So it means that when I lost interest about twelve years go, I could sort of do it with my eyes shut. It's an aptitude one doesn't lose. With the shop I thought: 'That's marvellous, I can live the sort of life I want, rent is terribly cheap, it can hardly fail to make money and I can go in once a week and dip my hand in the till. Walk out again. Lead the life of Riley.' Didn't quite work like that.

I was hoping it would have collapsed about seven years ago actually. I had a very good person working for me who I'd known for years and she inevitably decided that there were better things in life to do than work in a shop answering idiotic questions from tiresome people and making money for me, so she left and I absolutely couldn't find anybody to replace her, as good as her or as loyal, knowledgeable or charming so I had a succession of ghastly people working and a complete crook who more or less reduced me to bankruptcy, accumulated serious bad debts. I suddenly found myself with no assets, everything had disappeared. He went to Australia. Such money as I should have was locked up in a Belgian bank vault and I couldn't get hold of it. At that point I just thought 'Oh, sod the lot of you, I shall do something completely different' but it's wasn't easy to find something.

I still have writing novels at the back of my mind. I mean, if I were a novelist, I'd have done it by now. I think it's just a sort of excuse to put things off. I'd like to sort of get back in the film business but there's no money in it. I mean there are thousands of people on the periphery of the film business. If you're terribly keen you can get in making tea and sweeping the floor of the set, but that's not the way in for me. I did actually set up a film production company with a friend but it never got off the ground.

He's both a victim of his start in life and its beneficiary. He glides through life in a state of controlled panic, alternating between moments of high elation and desperation. The Micawber instinct sees him through.

Something will turn up. It usually does. I'm a great optimist but I'm extremely gloomy at the same time – impossible combination. I mean, I just don't worry about . . . well I do . . . but I certainly haven't until recently. I've convinced myself that something's bound to turn up.

For the last twenty years I've lived a life which is incomprehensible to anybody else. People go round I know saying 'What on earth's he doing? Must have masses of money' which I don't at all. I carry things to the edge of disaster. I think I must enjoy this. Yes, I must do. I mean, the number of times I've actually had to wait in an airport and the number of times I've *just* caught the plane. I've just been ski-ing in the Alps for the first time for twenty-eight years and I was incredibly foolhardy when I did it before and this time – it's a rather crazy thing to do at 47 – I was terrified. I just said 'I'm packing this in, I'd rather sit in a cafe and read a book than tear around showing off'.

I think I was very rebellious as a child but not in an overt way. I had my rebellions in the form of sort of bloody-minded, negative refusal to do things and then usually a realization that I actually had to do it, when I'd got five minutes to do it in. I was very successful at school. Obviously, I could have been much more successful. Really the fact that I could get away with it – I was clever enough to leave things to the last minute and do it better than everybody else – developed my Micawberish attitude now. I still think I can do some sort of amazing intellectual pirouette, but actually I'm sensible enough to know that's not so. I'm not as intelligent as I used to be. I know I'm not. Apart from some natural decay, I've probably drunk away half my brain.

He's partly 'stuck' because his 'rebellions' didn't free him from his background.

I suppose I've got rather involved in my family again, owing to the fact that my father is extremely old and senile. My mother's not senile, so I have to sort of take more interest in them than I used to. I mean I don't get on with my father at all, in fact I dislike him strongly, but I have to pretend to be nice to him because it relieves the burden on my mother. Always have got on well with her. My relationship with her is not sort of warm in an enveloping, maternal way but I like her and she loves me. It's terribly difficult to see it, trying to look at it from the outside. We don't see each other very often, never have done. I have a brother who's married and has children and is younger than me, leads a regular life and has a regular job, and the burden of looking after my parents somehow seems to have fallen on me. I have more time.

He sees his parents' marriage as fraught with difficulties from an early stage.

It's undoubtedly had an effect on me, and it still does. I'm not from a broken family but what seems to me to be far worse which is a family which should have broken up and didn't, which I'm constantly told by people explains the fact that I've never got married, because my earliest memories of marriage were unpleasant ones. I mean I really don't know why I never have got married. I greatly regret it and I think it's too late really. I've only thought that in the last couple of years, but I think it's probably unlikely that I ever will.

Much of his life is conducted on the basis that the future will somehow sort itself out. Now with time running out at midlife, he sees some of the doors closing, like marriage.

I wouldn't get married for the sake of it. I mean I can think of at least three friends of mine who at a certain period in life – I mean much younger than me – sort of thought 'Gosh I've got to get married, and I don't envy them or their wives. It's not the sort of thing I'd do. My taste in people doesn't lead me to be indiscriminate, it leads me to be more and more discriminate and I think it's very unlikely that I shall ever find the sort of person that I would want to be married to or that she would also want to be married to me. I mean, I'm just very very unlikely, statistically.

Which may be true.

I hadn't proposed marriage to anybody actually until I was about thirty or something. I mean I had lots of lasting relationships but I had a sort of familiar reluctance. I certainly changed my mind slowly but I'm very perverse about the sort of people I like. They are generally wildly unsuitable and wildly unlikely to want to marry me. In a sense I have an extremely romantic attitude . . . I follow my heart down several daft alleyways. Relationships with women are important to me, too much so I think. Well, there have been innumerable vicious circles that I've got myself in. I sometimes see myself just sort of walking in vicious circles.

The fact that I'm not really gainfully employed and only actually manage to keep things together by doing something slightly clever once a year that keeps me going for the next year. But I'm not by anybody's standards a success, and success is erotic. I mean I should be a weighty person at forty-seven and I'm absolutely the reverse.

I don't actually have any relationships with anybody at this moment which is a bad thing for me. The first time in my life I've ever actually not had one. I'm not used to it and I don't like it and the more I don't like it, the more impossible I become and the less likely I am to solve it or to end it. I become sort of wildly self-destructive . . . I mean, I actually like living with people but anybody else would say 'Yeah, Ok you like living with people but it's always on your terms.' I like the presence of company and conversation and all the rest of it, other people, a circle of friends that provide conversation. But that's not domestic warmth, that's something quite different. You don't really get to know a person until you actually live with them. All the pleasures that go with domesticity are quiet pleasures – rather than wild evenings sitting in restaurants drinking too much and making insincere passes at people.

I contemplate the future with a certain amount of dread which I never did before because I don't see any pattern and there has to be a pattern, otherwise I shall end up in a poor house, if such things still existed. I may not keep any friends; I may end up with no ties or anything else, which I certainly don't want to happen. The sensible thing to do would be to move somewhere else, but I don't like the idea. I've totally ruled out living abroad I think. Actually I've never ruled out anything completely. I wasn't born in London, I was born in the country and very much in the country. All my friends were children of farm workers during the war. I sometimes don't feel London is my home.

Mention of childhood brings out the nostalgia for the seamless existence of his early years which he tries at times to recreate. Money has always been a necessary adjunct of his life, and has sustained his lifestyle over the years. Now it's a worry.

Money is one of the reasons I actually feel middle-aged which I didn't feel three years ago. I feel money is really terribly important, which I never have done before. I've just made enough, spent it and never saved it. I am terribly poor actually by any real standards. I don't have an income and I've become sort of locked in a relationship with this fading useless business and I've got to make up my mind really, but I was saying that five years ago and I still haven't made up my mind.

On the pattern of my previous things, only imminent disaster would make that happen and it will probably happen in the next three weeks in the form of urgent messages on my answering phone from the Bank Manager. That is going to be it and I'm just going to have to say 'Ok, I'll sell it up lock, stock and barrel and pay off my vast debts' and then I will be tremendously relieved, but totally unemployed and unable to fall back on that. I've had endless thoughts about how to provide some kind of income. None of them are very practical because they all require money and I think I'm not the sort of person anybody would lend any money to. I mean, they would have done ten years ago but nobody in their right mind's going to lend me any money now.

I mean when I say to one or two friends 'For goodness sake, here I am, I'm not entirely without use, please suggest something for me' – mad idiotic ideas come up. I mean, I seriously thought with the person who lives upstairs (who is a complete opposite to me) of forming a publishing company. It's not by any means impossible, but we're so completely different that I'm not quite sure how it would work. And since the reason why we want to form a publishing company is because I want to publish the sort of books that I like and he wants to publish the sort of books he likes, we have endless disagreements about it. I know him very well and we just couldn't be more dissimilar.

He can't believe I'm as broke as I am, nobody can or maybe it's people with money can't understand people who don't have money. I have a very rich godfather. I had great expectations of him particularly when his son ran off to New Zealand and was never heard of again. He was sighted once in a sort of drunk state in a bar in Auckland or something. I thought 'God, now's my chance.' I got a letter from him about two years later saying . . . he was very very rich. He gave me some mumbo-jumbo about tax laws and how he was going to give me right now what he was going to leave me in his will. When I got to that I thought 'I can hardly bear to turn over the page and see what this is – millions of pounds', and it said 'I enclose a cheque for £3,000' which hardly made a dent in my overdraft and that was the end of that.

I'm sort of fascinated by the actual concept of middle-age which I now feel for the first time. I mean, it actually means something to me though I find it very difficult actually to say what I think about it. Physically one feels things not working as well as they used to, but in a sense I look upon it more from other people's points of view than I do from my own. I mean I lead an incredibly unhealthy life, and although it doesn't seem to affect me, I can see it from other people's points of view. It's a sort of sexual thing . . . I can see that I'm not nearly as attractive as I used to be, you know, one's teeth go yellow and grow apart.

He goes in for much self-scrutiny, difficult as it is for him to escape from the persona he has built up over the years.

I am goaded into action and behave responsibly if somebody else is involved, whereas if it's just me I know that I can behave badly within my own moralities. One of the things that I've noticed about myself since I've considered myself to be middle aged is that I have become self-destructive to a much greater extent and more irresponsible and frivolous, with both health and money. There is a sort of deathly gallows humour about it, I think. I even went into a clinic for alcoholism about eighteen months ago. That was a serious attempt to sort myself out. It involved total denial. That lasted about three weeks and I was frightfully good for another three weeks and then I just lapsed. I mean, this is something I really do have to do something about. I astonished practically everybody I knew by going in there – I'm not a sort of wild drunkard, you know. I don't sort of embarrass other people, it was much more a sort of interior thing, a refuge into which I fall. I just knew that I had an addiction to alcohol and some people were astonished that I went. Rather the reverse of normal thing which is to deny one's alcoholism while everybody else is saying 'you are'. I mean, I knew I was. I was fine there until they started throwing religion at me. I thought I can't spend most of my life thinking about things like that, mid-west American simplistic view of higher powers and I left. Somebody said 'Oh, why do you think he left?' and someone else said 'Oh, he was thirsty.' Succinct way of putting it, but she may have been right.

He has noticed since he turned forty that he's become interested in 'wholly inappropriate girls. It's my paternal thing perhaps; they're a wholly inappropriate age'. But it may be his way of descending the time scale and getting in touch with the 'lost' child in him that he's been dragging unconsciously behind all these years. It is an explanation, perhaps, of why his life has followed this pattern of fits and starts. He's seeking to do something about his existence now which he knows is in a perilous state and needs remedying. Midlife is a time of reckoning for him. He can't go on tilting at windmills forever. Beneath his Quixotic manner, he has an acute sense of time running out.

7

Transitions

Every man's condition is a solution in hieroglyphic to those inquiries he would put. He acts it as life, before he apprehends it as truth.

RALPH WALDO EMERSON

For the majority of men midlife stops short of crisis point. For them it is essentially a period of transition rather than transformation. The main thrust of their lives remains unaltered, there may be changes in emphasis, in orientation, a shift towards concern with home life and with improving domestic relationships. It's also the stage of life where men may look outwards towards their community or neighbourhood to offer their services in a altruistic way, a modified form of idealism. Again this may seem reminiscent of adolescence where idealism was a strong force, usually accompanied by a passionate attachment. Now the mood is a calmer one and the emphasis more on giving out.

Erik Erikson, the American psychoanalyst, defined this stage of life as a choice between stagnation and generativity. Stagnation represents going on with the same routines, using denial to combat the threat of change. Here a man is effectively marking time – at its worst this can become so strong a preoccupation with himself that he suffers 'the mental deformation in which he becomes his own infant and pet'. (On this same basis couples can develop a form of 'pseudo-intimacy' where they each indulge each other, and become each other's child.) Generativity means to embark on new ventures that draw out the latent wish to help and give back to one's fellow men. Teaching, in Erikson's eyes, was a good example of this with its focus on guiding the next generation and its linking up of adult, child and culture. Most adults 'need to be needed' and at midlife this can find an outlet in generativity, the capacity to give without expectation of return.

Erikson drew up an eight-stage view of the life cycle. Each stage presented a 'psychosocial crisis, a turning point, a crucial period of increased vulnerability and heightened potential.' How an individual handled that stage and its developmental tasks, or crises, determined his subsequent capacity to pass successfully through later stages. In other words, if he missed out on a stage or handled it ineffectively then this would make it doubly hard to negotiate the next point. Miss out on adolescence (where the key factors are identity versus identity confusion) and you're likely to have the problems re-surfacing at midlife. However, since each crisis point mobilises new energy and therefore affords an opportunity to rework previously unresolved issues, all is not lost. In his biographical studies of Luther, Gandhi and Einstein, Erikson shows how these repeating patterns appear in their lives and how for each of them midlife was a point of significant change.

Most of the interviews we conducted included transitional features of midlife, the shifts of emphasis in work and home life, the loosening of family ties as children grow older. For some men this is the launch of a period of self-actualization, a golden period previously blocked in early adulthood. Security, financial stability, the lessening of external pressures, their greater maturity allow them to exercise their judgment in choosing their way of life, often turning to new pursuits facilitated through an awareness of how to manipulate the environment and its resources. Such people give every appearance of being in command of their lives and view midlife as the transitional point to a second half of life.

In the case of Richard West his life has followed much of the pattern outlined above. Aware now of time left to live, he is seeking to move into new directions that had been missing or that are complementary to the life he has been leading.

Richard West is an advertising tycoon. A tall, rangy man, he's been outstandingly successful in his field, building his company up to being one of the foremost advertising concerns in the UK. Now aged forty-three, he views midlife as a time to consider changing course, expanding his horizons, and developing his altruistic side. He plans to enter Parliament, a move designed to give back, in some sense, to the society he's sought to fashion through advertising. As he talks, he's aware of missing elements in his life and the need for change. He spends most of the week in London but four years ago converted a barn in Gloucestershire and established a stud farm for brood mares, where he spends more of his time, in accordance with his changing and more reflective view at midlife. It's where this interview took place. He's married with three children. Beneath the middle class restraint and articulacy, you feel another person trying to emerge as he recalls memories of adolescence and paternal influence.

Most men see the half-way point in their lives as the equivalent of a menopause. They think they're running out of life and see the gaping grave some distance away and think 'Well, have they been on the planet for a good reason and done all the things that should be done on the planet?' We're only here once. Midlife makes you suddenly, for the first time really, conceive of actually disappearing, dying, going, and wondering whether you've spent your time here very well. And maybe having second thoughts about what you started doing twenty years earlier.

I certainly plan to change my career over the next decade. For the last few years I've been working in advertising and that's gone very well. I'd always, for the last five years anyhow, thought that I really wanted to get into politics. If you speak to me in ten years time and I'm still in advertising, well I won't be having a midlife crisis. I certainly plan to do something else. I want to be worn out, to quote George Bernard Shaw. So if there's any of me left, I shall be extremely disappointed when I'm put into the ground.

He enjoys his work still and keeps up a full schedule.

I'm lucky that what I do is fun, enjoyable for me every day. It fits in with the things that I am: very competitive and aggressive and reasonably quick-witted, able to shift from one thing to another. I've climbed most of the mountains in advertising, foothills rather than mountains and I'd like to do something else. In fact I'm reading a book now about Parliament or rather Parliamentary characters and I'm extremely interested in that. My wife says I simply want to stand on a bigger stage and shout at more people and she's probably right.

I've been in business for twenty-one years. This country will never become great unless we develop what I call a wealth-creating culture where people with talent go into business and don't just go into the professions or become civil servants or teachers. I want to get into politics and Parliament so that I can help companies and help create an environment where business can prosper not just in the south, but particularly in the north, which is an absolutely poverty-stricken area because it's been deprived of that culture.

If I don't get into Parliament, I'd plan to do something else. I don't relish any form of failure. There's only one career path failure I've had: when I didn't get my degree at Cambridge, which was for a string of reasons. Not being in Parliament, it wouldn't be the same level of failure because the chance of me getting in is about one in three. So to get in would be a great achievement. I've already fought one seat and did well but didn't win it and the next time round I would like to get a seat which I actually win. The problem simply is that with about 400 people applying for it, 20 will be taken seriously, of which I would now be one. Many of them will be younger than me, so if I get one for next time it will be good. I've got quite a lot of parliamentary and ministerial contacts which may help me but there won't be that many seats coming up which are winnable, and then after that, depending when the next election is, I'd be over fifty. Even though I could be a bundle of energy and enthusiasm, at the most I've got two elections ahead of me. My best chance is the next one. After that I'd do what I call the House of Lords strategy because that's the other way into Parliament and one of my present clients did it – so that's another way. Who knows? I haven't worked out the strategy for that.

I started as a copywriter, writing ads and wrote a book about advertising about ten years ago. Then, with three other people, I formed an agency and one of them turned out to be an absolutely brilliant businessman and he's really the guy who's been marketing us and taking us from a little London advertising agency to a fairly substantial worldwide group. I enjoy the struggles, the battle at different levels, but a lot of the time you're running a business that you're not in control of in the way that you would be of a small business. My job is to have to be a leader. I've never thought of myself as doing more than guiding people and creating a cultural environment. I write ads very occasionally; I enjoy writing ads but I don't do it very often, so you could say that I'm not doing all the things that I enjoy doing. One of the concerns I've had is that it would all come tumbling down at some stage so I think what drives one on to a degree is the fear, anxiety that if you don't do the right thing, it will all just disappear because business is built round people.

He's expressing a well-known midlife sympton: the fear of sudden collapse, of all previous achievement turning to nothing. It's linked to an awareness of time running out, with the inevitability of death at the end of the tunnel. The creative drive to build from nothing is strong in him. Sitting an exam at Cambridge was being ranked among others, one in the crowd, and that early brush with failure has clearly spurred him on to make his mark in the world in his own way. He's really an entrepreneur at heart, which allows him to capitalize on his strengths and delegate his weaknesses.

I mean, my pattern is I'm a great starter but a bad finisher. Like in the business, I'm good at winning a client, I'm not good at handling him or her, but I realize that and I've got very good people to do that for me. I think it's terribly important in life generally, in careers or whatever, you can very quickly work out what you're good or bad at. You need to find out what others are good at too and build on that.

Nowadays he welcomes the trappings of success:

It's nice to have a barn to sit in and horses to ride and all those benefits. It's good fun to have but I regard it as giant pocket money, not to be taken too seriously. I don't wake up at night screaming, because I was perfectly happy before all these things occurred. It wasn't 'how dreadful my life was'. I remember when we were first married going with my wife and buying clothes at Oxfam stores and things, and that wasn't terrible or awful. It's nice to have these grown-up toys, but it isn't about that. It's just that it would be very sad having built the company up and employing 3,000 people around the world, for that all to come to no good and crumble.

Hence his wish to make a more solid, lasting contribution through his parliamentary ambitions. He thinks back to his father and his influence on him.

My father was a soldier. I also see all these little battles to beat people one way or another in business as not dissimilar. Advertising is a fair enough environment to do that in, especially if you're competitive – it causes less harm than the army. The two biggest pleasures in advertising are to write a really good ad and to win a piece of new business by competing against other agencies and coming up with whatever ideas are needed, be they creative ideas or strategic ideas or client handling ideas, or just devoting energy to bounce somebody into your company rather than into some-body else's company. There is never more than a 5 or 10 per cent difference between winning and losing so you're always on the margin and that's great fun. When you actually win, you think 'great' and when you don't, you think 'Oh bugger – I'll find another one to attack.'

His father had expected him to follow him into the army, but he didn't want to get stuck in the middle ranks. Would getting into Parliament be a bit like being in the middle again, starting off as a new boy?

I don't think even as a parliamentary new boy it's like being a new boy. I think just being there you're not at the bottom of the ladder. You see, I don't mind being at the bottom of the ladder. What I mind is, say in the army, being at the bottom of a ladder in a mechanistic position. I mean, as a junior officer or a private or whatever, you basically always have to do all the things which you are told to do by other people. It is quite reasonable, because if people start shooting at you your instinct is to run away. Therefore all those individual instincts have to be programmed out of you. Starting at the bottom, that's alright. If you start at a place where you can be a vigorous new boy, that's great, because people throughout the world are crying out trying to find talent and they are looking for people with ideas and energy, which are two things I have, so that would be terrific. I don't mind those sort of challenges at all. It's the notion of having to be subservient to buffoons and unable to use one's abilities, to be locked into some nineteenth-century military discipline. That didn't excite me at all.

He sees party discipline as different.

You see, in the end it depends what your strategy is. I don't think I'd mind the concept of it terribly much. It's really like a package, so many things in life are a package deal. Very few things are perfect. I think it's quite reasonable. Party discipline is part of the price you pay for having the support of a party and with its name round your neck, you've a chance to get into Parliament. Without its name round your neck, with exactly the same beliefs, you don't, so that seems a reasonable ticket.

He's given some thought to the effect of his present job and possibly an MP's way of life on his family.

At the moment I spend too much time away from the family, more at the moment than I used to because now we've got a worldwide company. There is quite a lot of travelling to do – and I'm often away. Now, parliamentary things are an extra burden. If I want to get into Parliament, I've got to keep my profile reasonably high. There will be extra things I need to do between now and the next election which will take me away and if I do get into Parliament then you do work long hours in the evenings. So those are bound to be concerns of my wife. Her other concern is that she doesn't particularly want to go round opening fêtes and in fact when I stood for Parliament last time she was very un-keen on the whole thing but came up and was terrific once she got the hang of it. They liked her. You don't have to be a horsey lady to do these jobs. You can do it with softness and gentleness and niceness. Yes, it is a concern to her and in a way I'd prefer she would be happy to do that. For her, it wasn't obviously part of the deal when she first knew me. It's something that's been added on now and what I hope is that, if it happens, when it happens, she would or will find it ok. I think people are reasonably adaptable and I would have to do it in a way which was consistent with the family. I would not try to win a constituency that wasn't in range of here, because this is my home now more than my London home.

The significance of home and the value of family life increas in importance at midlife.

Whenever I'm in London, I'm off early in the morning and back lateish at night, whereas here I can sit down and fall asleep on the sofa, go out and ride my horses when I like. I'd sell my London house before I ever sold this. At the moment I've got a half-share in a plane and I'd swop it for half-share in a helicopter, so I could get up to my constituency on the Friday night to see people and be back here by the middle of Saturday to get at least two weekends out of four here. So that is the way I plan to be able to (a) be a better Member of Parliament and (b) have more time with my family. But it's not an easy one and I'm conscious I'm being a bit selfish, imposing my wishes on my family. But then I feel I've got something to contribute and if I don't do that, it will sort of fester away and not get used. One thing I tell my children is that the only sin, or rather one of the major sins, is to be given some ability by the Almighty and not to use it. I think it's a terrible waste.

He weighs up the physical changes at midlife.

I don't feel myself any older if I look at a photograph of me when I was twenty-nine than one of myself at forty-three. During an advertising campaign a few weeks ago, some colleagues suddenly saw this photo-graph of me and said, 'You look much better now' and I think I do. My clients pay more attention to me. I'm going absolutely bald. That generally doesn't worry me. I'm not disguising it, it suits me, so I don't worry about it at all. But putting on weight, as people seem to do, I don't like. I suppose I've still got this immortality thing. I don't see myself getting older in any way that I notice. Now, looking forward to age eighty, logically that can't be so, but I just see myself as a very sprightly eighty-year-old and I look round. My father's eighty-three now and spends six months in Portugal and six months in England. He packs into his six months what most people might pack into a year. I think if you keep yourself busy and active you don't actually slow down.

On the subject of immortality, had he any thoughts about after life?

No, no, you know when I get close to snuffing, I might persuade myself that there is one. If I thought I was coming back another time and that I'd come back in some form, depending on what it is, maybe I'd operate differently but I believe I've just got one shot. The lapel badge probably sums it all up which says: enjoy life – this is not a rehearsal. I wish, I wish I was able to believe in the whole dimension of religion and life hereafter. I think those that can are very lucky. It adds that extra dimension to their lives. I just found that my terrestrial logical mind can't make that leap, I'm unable to do that and that I regret. I would love to believe it. I read about a certain number of bright and intelligent people who have converted to Catholicism and I think that's an interesting thing but I can't see myself being able to make that leap, so I think I've only got one time round this track.

At his public school he found daily religion 'rather like cleaning your teeth'. It didn't really become something he was committed to, so for that reason:

. . . it dribbled out of my life – it never seemed to be offering anything relevant or helpful which is one reason why none of our children are baptised. We had the view, possibly wrongly, that we wanted them to make that commitment themselves – a bit naive really in hindsight, because unless there's religion with a parent, it's quite unlikely to happen.

He gets enormous pleasure from his three children.

I think kids are wonderful. I think it's great having kids around. Not because I don't like being on my own or just with my wife but I think that it is lots of fun . . . noisy little things challenging for warmth, love and affection for all their impossibilities and difficulties. I suppose I've a touch of Peter Pan-itis. I really don't want to grow up. I like the child-like things. When they are all grown up, I'm sure I will miss that. The way you actually can have a cascade of younger lives in your life, stimulating, enriching and challenging your own, is, I think, wonderful. I think being a grandfather is a very recommendable thing to be.

What you leave to your children in a personal sense, what they think, varies. My children say 'We don't want any of your money, we want to do it ourselves' which is nice. I'm trying to say I would be disappointed if they did low-profile, passive things because I suppose one way with your children is to perpetuate yourself and therefore if I see things that I recognize in myself in my children, I'm pleased for them to go out and compete and win and be victorious. If they chose to do the exact opposite, and there's no reason why they should be the same, I imagine I would feel that they weren't doing all they could with themselves. But then you see there's a difference. My life is built very much round the notion of doing things, whereas you can build your life round a notion of just being and exist in a much more peaceful way than the way I chose and get an almost Buddhist-like pleasure from every moment just by being present in that moment of time somewhere. I'm too restless an individual to get satisfaction from that but there's no reason why they can't do that, but I'm still unsure. I'd prefer to see them achieving and doing things than that.

There's a sense of continuity to his life. The transitions of midlife are a way of establishing new directions, while getting full value from the present.

I would love to think of our family having this house for centuries. I think it is a magical place. Not just because it's full of lovely people, but yes, that's a great fluke to find such nice people. It's a great set-up really because so many people seem to have been drawn to it. The last thing I would sell in my possession would be the barn and the children have loved growing up here. My grandmother had a house in Sussex – it wasn't a wonderful house but she'd had it for some time and I thought it was awfully sad when it was sold when she died. I'd love this to be a place which our children have. My father left the army just because he was worried about going all over the place. I was born in Pakistan and from there until I was about eight I'd been all over the place so I didn't have anywhere that I regarded as 'my home' in that sense.

Richard West's comments about new horizons at midlife find an echo in many of our interviewees who have been tied to one organization since first starting out in work in their early twenties. There's a wish now to move from what is felt to be a constricting environment to something more individual.

Alex Stewart, now forty-two, is a merchant banker who has been with the same company since he left Cambridge twenty odd years ago. He recognizes that what attracted him initially was that he would be part of a 'big, warm, smothering type of organization'. Now he's ready for a change. Indeed for him, as for many others in this book, there is a parallel between the wish to make this sort of job change at midlife and their own emotional and psychological development. We all carry around within us 'internal parents' as parental figures within our psyche. In early adulthood these are often constellated for a man as the figure of a little boy with his mother, with all the complexities of that relationship. The mother may be symbolized as a powerful source of care and protection and hence may lie behind the choice of job in a large, warm, protective organization.

By midlife a man may be ready to move on and assert his independence more, become less afraid of the mother within him and of her potential power to 'withold, devour and seduce'. He is ready to leave the large organization and strike out on his own. His working relationships may change to more collaborative or even subordinate ones with mother-type figures. Gone is the fear of being emasculated, released as he is from the internal mother figure. His work will reflect these changes and in time lead to a joining up of the values of work in terms of achieving, performing and thinking with those mostly associated with home: loving, caring and fostering. The ties between work and home life increase with an overlap of attitudes, and diminish the sometimes rigid divisions between them.

His more feminine side, to do with relatedness, may come into play more as he finds himself less subject to the 'tyranny of the internal father' (often represented in early adulthood by a need to prove himself in a 'masculine' way). This freeing-up of his sense of identity can lead to creative outlets beyond those of a traditional pattern. Work itself can move from being instrumental to becoming more creative. Too often creativity is seen in terms of artistic output whereas work itself, even such routine tasks as administration, can be just as creative to someone working to the level of their capability.

The next story shows a person who uses his activity as a therapist to monitor transitional changes in his own life. Joel Aston is an 'integrative therapist', an Adlerian emphasizing the three major life tasks of work, reproduction and friendship.

Once you're over thirty-five whether it's midlife crisis or midlife transition depends very much on the individual and what he's doing. I mean, I know people in their sixties who haven't yet come through a midlife transition, and others who go through it when they're nineteen or twenty and never really come out of it. My son's going through his own life crisis of change at fifteen and my thirteen-year-old daughter's been going through it since she was born. We've all got elements that stretch way back that may be part of the process of change, but then it firms up when you're older. There are things in my life, going back to when I was fifteen or sixteen, that were the beginnings of my midlife transition. They've only really become integrated later on. I mean things like personal deaths, traumas, that kind of thing, which happened then and then become integrated later.

The death of his sister aged eleven when he was sixteen marked him strongly and gave him a sense of urgency about life. He's developed this into the notion of 'rehearsal'.

The key for me of the idea of rehearsal was an idea I started to think about quite a bit in therapy with people. I mean, the idea is that it's no longer a rehearsal. This is actually it. This is the performance. It's no good continuing to rehearse, or thinking that you're rehearsing because you're actually performing. That's one of the major transitions in life.

The other day I read a film critic in *The Times* or *The Guardian* saying that only now that he was older did he actually get angry about wasting an hour and a half of his time watching a film he didn't want to see. When he was younger, he went into a film and if it wasn't very good, Ok he sat there, but now he got really angry. The same if he got on the tube train and it got delayed. I mean he was really angry that he'd lost ten minutes of his life and when he was younger the ten minutes didn't matter very much. That meant a lot to me, and connects with the idea of rehearsal, the idea that there is a limited span and that one should 'Stop messing, you only have a certain number of performances, so make sure you get it all in. Get the show on the road.'

He has applied this to his own life.

If I want something now, I tend to do it or get it, or buy it. If I want to go somewhere I go, because this is the performance and if you don't do it now, who knows, you could keel over next week, or in forty years' time, but there's no point in messing around.

The mention of death again shows how it presses in on his life.

I've gone through three major transitions which is probably three more than the majority of the population. I left school when I was sixteen absolutely determined I didn't want to stay at school. I was no good academically and what I wanted to do was to get out and work in journalism, marketing, advertising, that kind of feel. I did that, which went on for four or five years and then I thought I didn't actually want to do that at all; what I actually wanted to do was to be more in control of what I was doing and more creative so I started running my own business. It didn't really matter what the business was but I ran my own business for a number of years and that seemed Ok but then there came a time when I became dissatisfied with that and wanted to become more involved in other parts of my life that had been tinkering around in the background. So then I went through another enormous crisis – well, not 'crisis', almost challenge – when I started training as a counsellor and a therapist. I decided to close down the business, throw it all away, get rid of the house, the whole bit, and become a mini-cab driver, in order to do a degree of psychology. That was another enormous change. I did that and after ten years or so, I realized that I'd thrown out the baby with the bath water, because the bits I enjoyed earlier on, the creative part of setting something up and being self-motivated and all of that kind of thing and the adrenalin that goes with it were all missing.

His restlessness is compensated for by being able to work from home which brings him closer to his family, a definite plus at midlife. His father has just retired, leaving him to look after his elderly parents more.

They don't have very much money and they're not terribly competent in survival terms. So I'm having to take up responsibilities with them and I can see that increasing as the years go by. I don't think they're going to cope very well with old age, I don't see any signs that they will. I was unable to assist my father at all in the period leading up to retirement, regardless of the fact that I'd been involved in pre-retirement work for years, so he made absolutely no preparation and he went to work one day and the next day he went in and retired.

Responsibilities for his parents give him a sense of the life cycle, which he illustrates with two stories.

There's a lovely Talmudic thing that I found for my son and which he chose to read at his barmitzvah. It is the Talmudic story about a man walking in the park and seeing a very, very old man planting a tree and he says, 'Why should an old man like you be planting a tree?' The old man says, 'Because if my grandparents didn't plant trees, I wouldn't have had any shade.' And that to me is what it's about. It's not about something up there, it's about what we do here, how we live together and I believe in an after-life. The after-life is the effect of what we do while we're alive.

His other illustration is of how easy it is to miss out on what's really going on.

There's also the American film where the guy is about to kill himself when the angel pops up like a leprechaun next to him on the bridge, and says 'Why are you trying to kill yourself?' and he says 'Because life is worthless and I've achieved nothing' and the angel says 'Well, will you give me x hours of your time? We'll make the assumption you've never lived and then we'll go for a walk around the town.' He agrees to this and they go for a walk and they walk along past a cemetery and he sees a tombstone and it's his brother and he says 'Why is my brother buried here? Did he die?' The angel says 'He's dead. Well, of course you pulled him out of the water when he was drowning when he was six and you haven't been alive since. He's dead, I'm afraid.' He continues and then he sees this rather angry and tight middle-aged lady walking along the street, muttering away to herself and it's his wife and of course he never met her. And the film goes on like this . . . it's one of the classics.

Both these stories illustrate something of a life-cycle view of life that Erikson emphasized. The next two stories are of 'late starters' who link up with this cyclical view of life at a later stage than most. Yet often their delayed momentum means that midlife is a time when their hopes and expectations will come to fruition. In a later chapter we look at the influence of fathers on early adult life. For some the struggle with the father holds up their own development, so that it is only at midlife that they feel freed from this and begin to reach their potential and discover their individual abilities. This is the late developer syndrome, for whom midlife is still part of the journey rather than the point of arrival.

Anthony Hyde, now aged forty-seven, felt strong pressure during his early adulthood to join his father's publishing firm, which he had started, and eventually take it over. He was an only child, so the pressures were particularly strong. He resisted these expectations, as he felt it would give him little scope to develop his own individuality. Perhaps a characteristic of the only child is the urge to remain independent, so he chose his own path, in academic life and in scholarship and writing. Now at midlife he assesses the impact of these earlier decisions on his life. What are his feelings about going against parental wishes? Looking back it becomes clearer that the choice of career is often a means of dealing with parental expectations either by going along with them and therefore appeasing them, or rebelling against them. From midlife onwards a more individual choice can be made, in tune with one's perceived special abilities. For Anthony this centres on his writing a book he would feel justifiably proud of, vindicating his decision to step out on his own, but at the same time allowing himself to build bridges back into his father's world.

I started late. If I've got any career now it's as a result of a very late start. That was really when I was about thirty. In the writing field, to do anything good that really counts in your subject you ought to start as early as possible. In my case it was very late. But I feel I am still in a developing phase. Where career and publication and research are concerned I am now acutely aware, and this is probably a midlife thing as I wasn't aware of it earlier, that there are a lot of things that I haven't done and will never be able to do and that narrows my field of research very much. For example, I'm a lousy Latinist. This is a fact that has to be faced. A lot of people don't believe it when I say it but it's true. And that does mean that there is an enormous amount of literature which is closed to me as a historian and will remain closed and that is not going to get any better. I have no illusions about that whatsoever. In certain circumstances I can get by, I can more or less get the gist of it but frequently I absolutely can't get anywhere. And I'm working in a period in which Latin is very important. And this goes for certain philosophical currents which I'll probably never master. So that narrows one down very much.

In the field that I'm in, I suppose I haven't done too badly because I've made discoveries which nobody else has made and I've got a good memory and that enables me to make those discoveries because a lot of them were based on memory, on recognizing things. But it does remain limited. Another thing is if one can write fairly well one is in a very good position of strength *vis à vis* people who can't write so well but are much better scholars.

When he looks back over his life so far, he feels he is 'not sort of gnawed and miserable with remorse about the things that I haven't done in life' but one of the penalties of being a late starter is the comparisons to be made with contemporaries. This can have a double-edged effect. 'I honestly think a lot of my contemporaries have got further on. And rightly so. They started off far better. They started earlier. They organized themselves better. I have no particular regrets. By organizing themselves better and starting earlier they may have missed a lot of fairly important things which I've enjoyed doing.'

Holding back and waiting before launching himself can mean learning a lot by observing people 'and seeing just what they can do and what they can't do. Indeed what they can, and you can't, do.' Competition has never been a major factor for him, but it brings up the vexed question of maturity.

I feel a lot of people have got a maturity which I haven't got, are far more level-headed than I am. I imagine they're far more responsible than I am, though I don't quite know how to gauge my own responsibility. I just feel that people with children have a greater sense of responsibility. They're obviously going to be more tied down than I am by having children and having to think about the future. Having children also demands a certain generosity, a certain amount of giving, which nobody's ever demanded of me. But not having had children is not something that I regret.

Part of his getting away from parental ties has been to ensure a certain amount of freedom, above all the ability to travel.

I realize I'm in a sense much freer because I can travel when I want, to where I want. Travelling isn't a solution of course, it gets rather boring up to a point too; there's this frightful *déjà vu* aspect of travelling. One of the main reasons I travel is neither pleasure nor work, it's just to see whether I can still do it. With my Middle Eastern expeditions [where he goes for research] I am always scared stiff and that really is a challenge. I feel, as the years go by, rather cheated if I haven't done a Middle Eastern trip for the element of adventure but at the same time it's really sort of cushioned because it's not as if I go to the Middle East with absolutely no money and hitch hike across the Lebanon or anything like that. I don't do that. I go to Syria and stay in a comfortable hotel.

For a late developer, the period of preparation lasts longer. Now Anthony has a clearer sense of direction, of where his targets in life lie. These depend on the books that he would like to write:

Writing a book is one of the big markers for me. It encapsulates something and provides a sense of future. Books are a signpost to the future. The writer Alan Moorehead used to say that it was very traumatizing to see the unwritten page but I find the unwritten page absolutely marvellous, what's traumatizing is seeing what you've actually written. The unwritten page holds out promise.

From a career point of view he's now at a crossroads. Having been offered and taken up a university professorship which he recognizes as a 'peak', he is now in two minds whether to continue with it, or to split his time as he has done previously between two half university posts. There are echoes here of the main refrain in his life, his wish for freedom but also the wish to gain

credit in the eyes of the world which the professorship provides. It's very much a midlife conflict for him, the question of exchanging his long-cherished independence for the sake of worldly recognition, aware he might not be offered such a prestigious post again. Will this work against his chances of writing an acclaimed book?

In the end I'd always wanted to get credit in the eyes of the world through publication and not through an academic career. If I'd wanted that sort of credit more, I'd have gone about it in a different way. In my twenties, doors were being opened for me to go into my father's business. Thank God, I left that behind. I wanted to be free and of course the desire to be free has always played a very strong role in all my decisions. It may be quite an adolescent thing but it's something that I've always had. Adolescent because I feel I ought to be growing up, which takes us back to responsibility and having children. I might have reached a certain maturity in some areas, but this wish for freedom is not a sign of maturity. If everybody had my wish for freedom society would just fall to pieces, nothing would get done at all.

Yet the awareness of time running out is beginning to make itself felt.

Midlife for me means options being limited, or seeming as though they're limited. It's conceivable that I've got a greater choice now than I had ten or twenty years ago – then, I may simply have thought I had a greater choice. Now I think I'd certainly be very hesitant to throw up anything indiscriminately. I'd make sure I kept something else lined up. I've even started worrying now about pension possibilities, things like that, it's not a consistent worry but it's become important because one sees now what happens to people who haven't worried about it – they're left without any money whatsoever in their fifties, and nothing to look forward to. I've always tended to look to people older than myself as role models. When you're in your late forties, the people older than you are considerably older, and you see how they live. After sixty-five it gets rather nasty. So I would say health and money are two factors that count, but even more important is companionship. Certainly companionship without health or money wouldn't be that rewarding and I'm very aware now that I'm growing closer to my wife in a very real sense. It's part of an overall change in emphasis, this question of closing options.

Recently the prolonged last phase of his father's life and his death at the age of eighty-eight made him reflect on growing old, 'the sight, the presence, the growing intimacy with old age,' though the actual death of his father had less impact on him than he expected.

Its main drawback must be physical decrepitude. Because you can't do the things that you would have done otherwise. Even now I notice I just get tired more quickly, have less energy. Old age can be unpleasant, humiliating, poor, miserable, cold. I wouldn't say his death was an event that marked me at all. No, it was more seeing my father grow very old. Actual death, no. His growing old was like a sort of forerunner of his death and in a sense, much worse. I wouldn't like to be like that. Death isn't something I think that much about. I sometimes think of the possibilities of, as everybody does at some point, the easy way out, which one probably shouldn't take. But in some cases one might. Suicide I'd only use if I found I'd manoeuvred myself into a really impossible situation. Then I would imagine suicide being rather nice and useful. I think it's probably an indication that I'm at heart still an adolescent.

The mention of suicide and adolescence shows how midlife revives many of the same dilemmas and questions of identity. Anthony has always tried to keep a close control over his life ('I'm not sure there was a period when I really didn't know myself fairly well'). Having 'made it in my own way', did he feel any sense of guilt towards his father for rejecting his plans for him as his son and heir?

Absolutely not, no. Not for a second. My father was rather good about that. Originally he did all he could to sort of force me to do it. Then when he realized I wasn't going to, he was generous, he was imaginative, surprisingly, because he wasn't necessarily always either one or the other. He suddenly realized that it wasn't the thing for me, then he accepted it completely. This was I suppose when I was in my mid-twenties. And he never reproached me with it. All he ever did was to tell me how right I was not to have gone into publishing and I think really that was very generous.

On the other hand the fact that his father never seemed to take a real interest in Anthony's own career has rankled.

He rarely asked me about the books I was writing or he might ask me but he wouldn't even pretend to understand. And that was something I was rather surprised about. He had no idea of how the academic world worked and it didn't interest him. The only thing that he understood was how books sold. If I wrote a book that sold and my book on Fascism did sell, by that he was very favourably impressed. The books I've written since weren't sort of intending to sell, they didn't sell, and by that he wasn't impressed. He was judging me from his own perspective. I was setting out on a different path, a more difficult path, not making use of the props that I could have got from him and his world and he could have taken more interest in that, as he was something of an entrepreneur himself. It was a necessary course for me to take. It's partly being an only child. I don't know how other only children have dealt with it. I felt stifled but then I think that my parents were particularly stifling parents. The idea of having to have breakfast with my father in the morning and then go in his car to his office and work for him all day, which was how it was really served up to me, was extraordinary now looking back, and with my mother there to say goodbye and be there when I came back.

He felt he had to escape from that straitjacket but the consequent lack of interest in his own career has left him feeling 'dissatisfied'.

I suppose that's part of human existence. One can't have everything. And you know since it is fashionable nowadays to blame the parents' reaction, why not do it? It's made me clearer in my mind that my ambition is to write these books. What I'd like most is to see these books in a shop window in London. And to think 'Ah, I've done it.' And then I really would feel I'd made it.

The fact of his father's death seems to have been a significant turning point in his life. It's partly released him to pursue his own interests more. In the next story the death of the father plays an equally important part.
   Barry Hanson, at forty-eight, has chosen at midlife to extract himself from the normal working world. It's partly by design, partly to do with pressing subconscious reasons, the wish to establish freedom and lead an unencumbered life. The death of his father three years ago was a significant moment:

It triggered my midlife changes off, because I think I wasn't all that far down the road with some of these ideas then. Up to the age of about eighty my father had never grown up from being about eighteen. He'd always been fit and he'd always been somebody who, although I didn't understand it in that way, was a great exponent of the 'being' model. Mother was much more ambitious and more successful. They'd never had a holiday together for thirty years because of work pressures. Then he retired and they enjoyed ten years together and then father got ill and he became a total demand on her.

Perhaps there's a fear that history may repeat itself with him if he stayed too long in full-time work. His father had always taken the view that 'there was nothing after death', but when it came down to it,

. . . he was very frightened of dying and it was very disconcerting to see. As long as he was totally healthy he never gave it a second thought, but as soon as he started losing his eyesight and having problems with other parts and becoming physically conscious of his mortality, it was a very nervous vicious circle. Yet when he actually died, although he'd been ill for a while, my memory of it was of a very powerful sense of at-oneness and peace.

In this experience of his father, with the fear of dying mixed to a sense of oneness, Barry had forged the constituents of his present way of life.

In many ways I'm very lucky because I don't have a family, a wife and two kids in the suburbs, nor a mortgage, nor economic pressures, I have what I would call survival pressures. Many of the issues with regard to male changes in midlife come from work. People get to the point of saying 'Is there more to life than working to live?' I don't have those pressures and those commitments and in many respects I have a lot more freedom of options. The core issues are 'What's life really about?' If you've been under domestic pressure with two kids and a mortgage and a wife, that can be very traumatic, or if you're used to working for the same company for twenty years, with all your support systems related to the company, or if in addition you've been brought up to believe that that's the only thing to life, that can be even more traumatic. I find I can't use those sort of measures anymore and get my identity out of them. I needed to ask 'What else is there? What have I missed out on? Aren't there other things in the world?'

He started life 'originally in that pattern' and in his early thirties was married for three years which gave him some awareness, practical awareness, of what that other world is about.

I've moved in and out of the corporate world quite a bit. The last permanent job that I had was with a large international company in the North-East. I commuted from London for two days every week as my job was a link between the new business developments there and the financial/venture capital section in London. Then they reorganized and my job disappeared. I'd become a corporation person and once you're that, you're part of their network of people but I didn't want to go and live in the North-East. I had enough economic security to be able to say 'Well, it doesn't worry me too much whether I have a job or not. I can do what interests me.' I happened to be the Chairman of an Association which was a full-time hobby anyway, and that meant there was an office to go to.

What also happened, it was a coincidence really but particularly relevant to all this, was that I spent a month in Nepal at Christmas and another month out there again at Easter, and I also went to Tibet. That experience was very reinforcing in a way, and very compatible with the idea that I'd been stuck, trapped in a fairly stressful 'go-for-it' world. I happen to think that most of the problems that you come across are stress-related problems concerned with coping with the world that we're living in. A lot of that actually comes down to, in very glib terms, the 'go-for-it' model. Everybody's living in the future with ambitions, with success, with all the stress-related pressures. It so happens that the experiences that I had were very eye-opening about the alternative which is the 'flow-with-it' model, in other words the actual being rather than going for it. I suppose I should have been much more aware of earlier, but for all sorts of historic reasons – to do with essentially family pressures, university education, moving into technology and then to business school – I wasn't.

The success model is the acceptable model that comes out of most of our educational system. Getting married is part of that. Women aspire to success too, but historically it's been difficult for them to do it independently. They've aspired to it by proxy and that put pressure on males. One of the reasons why I believe that there's a 'crisis' point corporately for a lot of males is that having moved fairly fast in their thirties, they reach a plateau in their forties and the challenges aren't there. They have been by-passed, younger people are coming along. That causes enormous troubles with their partners because partners have been using the identity issues of the male in order to establish their identities.

In his own case he recognizes he is 'a late developer'.

I'm not very prone to settling down in the traditional pattern for maybe deep-seated insecurity reasons. Coming out of my own marriage may have been more deeply rooted in other factors, maybe unresolved issues with the relationship with my mother or family relationships that made it very difficult to cope with settling down in that traditional model. Also, I became aware on reflection that I married somebody who was in love with the idea of being married and I was in the wrong place at the wrong time.

His midlife dilemmas revolve around this pull between setting up his own life or being part of the 'established pattern'.

There is a legacy of expectations, I think, that is quite difficult to come to terms with. It's a very conflicting legacy between the legacy of success in traditional terms, which is thoroughly dependent on the outside world, and the other element of almost wanting to opt out of all that and just be in total control of one's own life. I think it's in many ways a very paradoxical conflict this. Some people are able to 'flow' with that success model, probably because of family backgrounds and possibly to do with the class structure. They seem to have a naturalness. I suppose still there are pangs of jealousy, envy that you can't – that I can't – have everything, and there are still naive childish fantasies that you can actually do everything and have everything.

Midlife revives nostalgically some of the fantasies of omnipotence previously experienced in childhood.

In a sense I've got that because I've got choice and control over ninety per cent of what I do with my life. I haven't got anybody else to be accountable to. It feels like success and, in a sense, it is success but if you're put into a peer group dinner party and someone says 'What do you do?' You can't very well say 'I be'. You could try, but they'd be all so threatened by it. They'd be very defensive, if not antagonistic, and you'd better become something – some other label – just in order to play with them. Labels are part and parcel of everyday life. Today I went to a computer exhibition and I find it very annoying where you turn up at these booths to check in and they say 'Can you give me your company name please?' and I say 'I haven't got a company name.' I almost feel that I want to walk out, until they list people under their individual names. I think it's not only bad psychologically for everybody to get so corporatized, it's actually going in the wrong direction, because the next decade or so will be on much more of a wave of the individual.

He is still only half-way to where he would like to be philosophically but he feels he is getting there.

Increasingly over the last ten or fifteen years, I've had a very powerful awareness of nature and the patterns and the power of the universe, partly through taking photographs. It's told me a lot about the way in which nature and the nature of the universe are a mutual manifestation of each other. Being, in the sense I've described, is making yourself an integral part of nature to the point that it actually doesn't matter whether you're alive or not. It may sound a bit quasi-Buddhist, but if you can at least take that on board, it does mean that death is much more of an integral part of life, and life after death then is less of an issue. It's just a different state of being.

8

Creativity

To be creative means to consider the whole process of life as a process of birth, and not to take any stage of life as a final stage. Most people die before they are fully born. Creativeness means to be born before one dies.

ERICH FROMM

When your Daemon is in charge do not try to think consciously. Drift, wait and obey

RUDYARD KIPLING

Creativity is in everyone's gift. There's a tendency to assume that only 'creative' people (artists, writers and so on) are capable of truly creative work. Yet as the quotation above by Fromm shows, creativeness informs all aspects of an individual's life. Day-to-day work such as business, much maligned for its materialistic approach, or government and administration can all be creative in the use they make of an individual's capacity, his judgment and use of discretion.

It's hard to find a satisfactory definition for creativity, the usual one being 'the ability to bring something new into existence'. Yet there's something mysterious about it as well, the result of the interplay of conscious and unconscious forces, traditionally the ground where artists of all sorts have drawn their inspiration.

How do 'creative' people, in the accepted sense, experience midlife and what special significance has it for them? Elliot Jaques in his paper 'Death and the Midlife Crisis' studied this problem with particular interest and came to the conclusion that three avenues opened up for creative people at this juncture. There was either a drying-up of the creative ability (the so-called writer's block); or there began a period of creativity that might well last through old age (Cervantes, for instance, wrote Don Quixote at sixty); or as a third possibility, a notable change would take place in the quality of creative output, a more mature, reflective attitude emerging, sometimes subdued, sometimes 'resigned', even playful – as can be found, for example, in Shakespeare's last plays or Beethoven's late quartets. This he termed 'sculpted creativity'.

For most people, midlife offers the chance to catch up with creative paths that have either been missed out on earlier on, or relinquished, by force of circumstance. The novel that someone was always promising to write or the painting ability that has lain dormant all those years may now flourish. We see evidence of this in the number of people enrolling on Open University courses or going to adult education centres to acquire new skills. Earlier we saw how Bill Mason hoped to go to Art College once he'd retired and John Newton planned to try his hand at writing, something he hadn't done since his early twenties. In both cases the activity is undertaken as much for its own worth and enjoyment as for the wish for acclaim. The second half of life is concerned with the sense of interior fulfilment and satisfaction, as much as public, outside recognition.

Midlife is a turning point, a time when a writer or artist is beginning to ask himself serious questions about what he has achieved so far and whether the 'pattern on the carpet' will remain forever the same, whether he will ever achieve a masterpiece. Or it may clarify his mind as it does for Anthony Hyde who knows now that his one remaining ambition is to write a book that he will be remembered by. Scott Fitzgerald came to a clearer understanding of his true nature as a writer after undergoing a midlife crisis when his writing career and personal life ended up on a collision course and teetered on the brink of disaster as he graphically described in *The Crack-Up*.

As a young man Scott Fitzgerald seemed to have everything, 'all that the world affords, fame and prosperity, work and play, love and friendship', as one commentator put it. A best-selling author at twenty-three, he wrote *The Great Gatsby* in 1925 aged twenty-nine and *Tender is the Night* in 1934. He seemed to be identified with the Jazz Age, 'it bore him up, flattered him and gave him more money than he had dreamed of, simply for telling people that he felt as they did', as he described it later.

His marriage to Zelda started off as the stuff of dreams, the world captive at their feet. In New York they wandered about 'like children in a great bright unexplored barn' and, at the height of his fame 'riding in a taxi one afternoon between very tall buildings under a mauve and rosy sky, I began to bawl because I had everything I wanted and knew I would never be so happy again'. Such a romantic view of life was bound to have its come-uppance, the ingredients for a midlife crisis already taking shape. 'Sometimes I don't know whether I'm real or whether I'm a character in one of my own novels.'

By 1935 he was thirty-nine and matters were coming to a head. He had a recurrence of a serious illness (tuberculosis) he'd suffered briefly in College.

Zelda was by now committed to an institution he was struggling to pay for; he was forcing his talent writing magazine articles; his drinking had worsened; debts mounted up. So many factors combining triggered off a crisis. He cracked, 'like an old plate cracks'. Overwhelmed by the feeling that he had wasted his abilities through 'an over-extension of the flank', a burning of the candle at both ends, he contemplated a bleak future. Insomnia haunted him. 'In the real dark night of the soul, it is always three o'clock in the morning, day after day.' There was no escape, no hiding place.

He tried one last fling, left his home in Baltimore with seventy cents in his pocket and took himself off to an unknown town in North Carolina and checked in at a cheap hotel. He stayed there for two days living off tinned meat and soda crackers, washed down with two cans of beer. He tried to write a short story to pay his hotel bill, but it was no good. Returning home again, he knew his crisis was upon him. It was a 'blow that comes from within – that you don't feel until it's too late to do anything about it, until you realize with finality that in some regard you will never be as good a man again.'

He wanted to be 'absolutely alone' seeking an 'insulation from ordinary cares' and a loosening of the bonds of his everyday life.

> It was not an unhappy time. I found I was good and tired. I could lie around and was glad to, sleeping or dozing sometimes twenty hours a day and in the intervals, trying resolutely not to think. I made lists – made lists and tore them up, hundreds of lists: of cavalry leaders and football players and cities, and popular tunes and pitchers, and happy times, and hobbies and houses lived in and how many suits since I left the army and how many pairs of shoes. And lists of women I'd liked, and of the times I had let myself be snubbed by people who had been my betters in character or ability.

His crisis was going through recognized stages, now part of a gradual disassociation from the past, almost playful in its reversion to child-like habits, of reverie and list-making. He was full of introspection, of self-examination.

> I began to realize that for two years my life had been drawing on resources that I did not possess, that I had been mortgaging myself physically and spiritually up to the hilt . . . that every act of life from the morning toothbrush to the friend at dinner had become an effort. I saw that for a long time I had not liked people and things, but only followed the rickety old pretense of liking. I saw that even my love for those closest to me was become only an attempt to love, that my casual relations – with an editor, a tobacco seller, the child of a friend, were only what I remembered I should do, from other days.

Now came the hardest part, becoming 'an unwilling witness of an ex-
ecution, the disintegration of one's personality.' He stood at his cross-
roads. The choice lay between a return to his former self with the likelihood
of self-destruction through drinking, or accepting the nature of his crisis,
confronting it head-on with clear mental resolution. 'When I had reached
this period of silence, I was forced into a measure that no one ever adopts
voluntarily. I was impelled to think. God, it was difficult! The moving
about of great secret trunks. In the first exhausted halt, I wondered whether
I had ever thought.' He thought back to his past, to the dreams of his youth,
on how he had missed out on the Princeton football team and had buried the
hurt for years, as he had the mixture of shame and rejection he had felt on
not getting to fight in Europe in World War I. These suppressed memories
from his youth now re-surfaced to haunt him. His past was catching up with
him, and he was reliving it.

He needed to detach himself from the persona, or false self, he had worn
for years. He noted how in the intervening years he had often identified
himself with 'the objects of his horror and compassion'. Now he would 'slay
the empty shell' and discover a truer self. He would concentrate on what he
knew he was good at, being a writer, cutting out all other distractions and
becoming much tougher on himself and on others. 'I would cease any
attempts to be a person – to be kind, just or generous. There was to be no
more giving of myself.' It was a decision that made him feel 'rather
exuberant' giving him a 'heady villainous feeling' as the transformation
took place, freed at last from guilt and duty-bound obligation.

His new self was in sight. 'I have now at last become a writer only. The
man I had persistently tried to be became such a burden that I have "cut
him loose" . . . The old dream of being an entire man in the Goethe-Byron-
Shaw tradition . . . has been relegated to the junk-heap.'

From this 'second act' in his life (he'd once written a famous phrase that
there are no second acts in American lives), much creative output flowed.
The letters he now wrote to his daughter Scottie demonstrate this. They
have a firmness and sense of purpose hitherto missing in his life. 'I wish now
I'd never relaxed or looked back,' he wrote to her 'but said at the end of *The
Great Gatsby*: "I've found my line, from now on this comes first. This is my
immediate duty – without this I am nothing."' With his new-found
realism, he wanted to express to her 'the sense that life is essentially a cheat
and its conditions are those of defeat, and that the redeeming things are not
"happiness and pleasure" but the deeper satisfactions that come out of a
struggle.' And later, with not misplaced compassion about himself, 'I am
not a great man but sometimes I think the impersonal and objective quality
of my talent and the sacrifices of it, in pieces, to preserve its essential value
has some sort of epic grandeur.'

He had come through his crisis, enhanced. From this position of renewed
writing vigour, he produced *The Last Tycoon*, his last, and arguably his

best, work before his sudden heart attack and death in 1940 aged forty-four.

The fear of writer's block or its equivalent haunts most creative people at midlife. The first flush of success, of 'easy lyricism', may have achieved a certain amount of fame. Now the fear of the source of inspiration drying up, creative flow stopping, having nothing left to say haunts the creative person. In his film *8½*, Federico Fellini shows a successful film director at mid-career assailed with doubt and uncertainty as he is about to make his next film. Images from his past, from his youth at his Catholic school, of being punished and going to confession, of being put to bed by his grandmother, of running off to the beach to peep at the grotesque female who lives in a shack there, mingle now with dreams of restored omnipotence, the confusion of his present life, of his personal relationships, of getting his wife and mistress to meet together in the same café. Chronic indecision as people pester him for parts in his forthcoming film. The recurring image, his 'lost' inspiration, is of the circus. Towards the end of the film, as he makes his way to the space age set for his new film, besieged by journalists questioning him about his beliefs and intentions, he attends a press conference. When the producer of the film introduces him and whispers in an aside for him to speak, he can't do it and crawls under the table on the dais and runs away. On the periphery of the set he encounters the circus troupe of players. Suddenly he is restored again as ringmaster, inspired again to direct. The troupe starts to perform and the other key personages from his past descend the staircase through a curtain to join in. Past and present have come together and he can start afresh.

Such a story encapsulates the artist's dilemma at midlife. Some feel 'stuck' and hopeless.

August 30th: morning tears return; spirits at their lowest ebb. Approaching forty, sense of total failure; not a writer but a ham actor whose performance is clotted with egotism; dust and ashes; 'brilliant' – that is, not worth doing. Never will I make that extra effort to live according to reality which alone makes good writing possible; hence the manic-depressiveness of my style – which is either bright, cruel and superficial; or pessimistic; moth-eaten with self-pity.'

Cyril Connolly, *The Unquiet Grave*

Experienced writers often get round writer's block by a strong technique. Graham Greene sets himself a target of 750 words a day, if more or less he aims to rectify it the next day. Hemingway, having sharpened ten pencils before starting to get himself going, wrote from dawn till one o'clock, standing up at a high desk, always stopping writing for the day at a point where the writing was going well and he knew what was going to happen next, so that he could continue with it the next day. Willa Cather read the

Bible for an hour before starting each morning. Such strategies are designed to maintain flow and continuity, and are marks of self-discipline and craftsmanship, the homage the conscious mind pays to its unconscious counterpart when it's threatening not to deliver.

Yet the fear that midlife brings about the drying-up of creative ability is often hard to dispel.

Edward Carter is forty-two years old and has worked both on stage and in television. In a paradoxical way, for all his midlife anxieties he's happier on the stage: 'You're far more in control of what's happening on stage.' But the stress he feels elsewhere is beginning to affect his work. He finds he has to work 'that much harder' at acting – 'so consequently when I fail at something or when something doesn't quite work as I want it to, I feel desperate.' He's tempted to seek another direction, re-train as a director or cameraman. He wishes he had thought of that ten years ago when he was younger. 'If you fail when you're younger you've got a chance of picking yourself up. I seem now to have a total lack of self-confidence. It's a constant struggle with me just trying to prove that I can do things.' He describes the identity confusion an actor begins to feel at midlife: he is so used to taking on other roles that he's not sure of his own identity and feels he can only be somebody when impersonating them as an actor.

I sometimes wake up in the middle of the night or suddenly stop myself in the car and think 'God, in ten years time I'll be fifty-two, and that will be it really. I feel very down at times saying to myself "Christ, what have I achieved?" Not a great deal. If I were to drop down dead tomorrow, people would say "Well he did a couple of telly programmes and if you want to see him he's preserved on video." But it's not much of an achievement really.'

Roger Holmbury is a TV documentary film-maker with some thirty or more films behind him. Aged forty-three, he's reaching a turning point in his career.

The main reason for being a documentary maker is to try and communicate to others your excitement at seeing something for the first time yourself; in your arrogance, or naivety, you imagine that since you've just seen it for the first time, an awful lot of people will never have seen it or had thoughts about it. Now I worry that this urge is going to diminish as time goes on. For instance, I've just been to Calcutta and it's meant to be the ultimate experience but I find it's no longer very surprising. I've seen enough like it in Delhi, Beirut, Bombay or wherever. Of course it is different, but it isn't different enough for me to get a big charge about it and say 'Jesus, I must tell everyone about it, tell them what it's like.'

It makes me think I'd better find something else to do. This must be what this midlife thing is all about, thinking it's time to change and go in some completely different direction. I've made some thirty documentary films. Over the years you learn techniques and you carry around with you an increasing number of them, so everywhere you go begins to remind you of some other film you've made. It becomes less of a challenge, less difficult to pull off, and you worry about repeating yourself. So you think you better do something that's new and really scary. Trying to write a feature film could be a possibility as it's unknown territory and would involve a whole load of new skills, as well as an extension of existing skills. Being a documentary-maker you're basically a parasite on other people's lives and a feature film allows you to invent a world of your own.

But the problem is, how do you start something new when obviously you're running down and your physical resources are becoming less? When I look back on it, I see the first thirty years as being on a sort of curve for twenty years, then you move onto a plateau for the next ten or fifteen years. After that, wear and tear and inevitable biological deterioration mean that you're going to be less able to keep it up. I've been making films for fifteen or twenty years – probably for the first ten of them I was physically and mentally quite keyed up and fit, now deterioration and the feeling of getting older are much more evident. It's the idea of going through the same routines that's off-putting. It's just conceivable I might have another thirty years ahead of me, a long time, but I've got the feeling that I already know what it's all like, I've been to this place and that, talked to this person and that. Everything becomes a bit like something else you've seen before. This bothers me, makes me wonder how I'm going to keep some sense of adventure and momentum going, find something that's exciting enough to get out of bed for, when it may all be just a variation on known models.

What also scares me is the idea that as you grow older you simply don't realize or notice that what you may think of as being acute or perceptive of you really isn't anything of the sort. Other people may notice it, but you don't. Younger people may already be seeing that your self-perception, your own valuation is way off the mark. I can remember when I was younger meeting older people who gave the impression they knew what they were doing but I could see they were over the top. What if that was to happen to me?

Misgivings about the quality and originality of creative work apply just as strongly in other fields. A writer may feel he has nothing new to say, he's repeating the same patterns. Graham Greene put this well:

Writing a novel does not become easier with practice. The slow discovery by a novelist of his individual method can be exciting, but a moment comes in middle age when he feels that he no longer controls his method; he has become its prisoner. Then a long period of *ennui* sets in; it seems to him he has done everything before. He is more afraid to read his favourable critics than his unfavourable for with terrible patience they unroll before his eyes the unchanging pattern of the carpet. If he has depended a great deal on his unconscious, on his ability even to forget his own books when they are once on the public shelves, the critics remind him – this theme originated ten years ago, that simile which came so unthinkingly to his pen a few weeks back was used nearly twenty years ago in a passage and so on.

At midlife the influence of the outside world begins to impinge more. Family changes, physical strains all intrude on the creative process. Hitherto many creative people have managed to keep the two separate, maintaining the privacy of studio or writing study apart from the hurly-burly of domestic life. The doubts and uncertainties that are inescapably part of midlife have to be taken on board. They can and should be incorporated into the new output, fulfilling in that sense Jaques's third category (see page 107).

Neil Marlowe is a writer, with a special interest in radio drama. Aged forty-seven, he's a stockily-built, good-looking man, with a grizzled beard, full of intensity and intelligence. He speaks rapidly, his mind racing ahead of his words, full of expletives like 'Whoopee!' and 'God's strewth!' He lives in Barnes with his wife. They have two children, a son who has just left home and gone to sea, and a daughter aged sixteen who is still at school.

Midlife is a time for lot of changes. I've been thinking about it. It's things like kids leaving home, hopes, dreams and ambitions not being achieved. It's finding yourself and coming to terms with certain things: – watching parents grow old and die, or whatever. It increases your awareness of those things.

The interview was in his book-lined attic studio, with pictures on the walls, some framed, some just stuck up, an ethnic rug on the floor, frequently interrupted by the noise of planes overhead. He talks freely of midlife issues. As a dramatist he's used to tuning in to the undercurrents in people's lives.

I've just done a whole group of plays about health-related problems, about health education, cancer, with a commercial radio station. About how parents cope with finding out their kids are heroin addicts, how you deal with your first heart attack. I mean jolly subjects! But doing the research for those you come against people the same kind of age as you with the same kinds of hopes and dreams and expectations and they are suddenly faced with something which is absolutely shattering and you suddenly realize how fragile the whole thing is. I mean, the whole of their world just crumbles, you know. The woman who's the mother of a guy who is a heroin addict said to me that I had no idea what it was like to want your child to die every time he walked through the door. I just find it shattering to carry that kind of load, and when you come away from it you are carrying it too, and the work you do is related to it.

Perhaps it is no accident that he has chosen these heavy-weight subjects at this juncture in his life, to tie in with his own preoccupations with the shortage of time and the inevitability of death – always the invisible sub-text of midlife re-evaluation.

I've just finished a play about AIDS which had the aim of removing the kind of demonology about it and the kind of myths that have been brought on around it, so that people can actually approach it for what it is, which is terrible and frightening, but doesn't require you to not drink out of someone's cup or not kiss or whatever. And talking to blokes, men who are six months into it and finding them to be nice people and knowing they are going to die and you write a play about this and you're using them, and they know you're using them and they appreciate why you're doing it, it's a very intrusive business.

Necessarily intrusive though, as midlife calls for themes that are close to the bone, themes of death, survival, sudden change (cancer). By mobilizing his own anxiety so that he can hold it up to examination, Neil can work through some of his fears through his writing.

Writing *is* an intrusive business really, I have always thought this. It's sometimes hard to carry on. Doing the research for the drugs thing, I became paranoid about the whole thing. That permeates the whole of your family and that's not good, but it's very hard to divorce the work, which is why I do it I suppose, from going to the supermarket.

In other words, work and family life merge more at midlife. He is trying to organize a surprise birthday party for his wife at the moment.

Of course she's aware, and of course she knows, but we keep this myth going just for fun. That's all part of reappraising those relationships too, in a sense. With the kids going, you start to talk to each other again and you haven't talked to each other properly for years. What's comforting is actually to say to somebody else who's got kids the same sort of age as ours and hear them say 'Oh Christ, yes, we've got the same problem. You know, we have probably half an hour a week really on our own, where we want to just talk.' Maybe it's more than that, but it seems like that. Your life takes off in different directions, and if you're both working there are sets of values and sets of friends which are separate so you kind of separate out, then the kids start to go and you suddenly realize 'Christ, if it's going to work for the rest of your life, you've got to find a way of making it work' and that's exciting in a way. I mean, that's fun because it's going back to square one. It's what you have got before the kids were around.

It needs courage to go on and confront this.

I think it's very easy to 'cop out' at this stage. I'm in a business where people cop out all the time. Though most of my friends haven't, oddly enough, gone through that kind of routine divorce. I think many of them have been through the reappraisal or are going through it. I guess most of the men in my business are, in one way or another, writers, directors, producers and actors and we all have the same belief that we were going to be the best. But, if you don't believe that, you don't do it – there's no point. I mean, it's too hard, it's too damaging, it's stupid. That's overstating the case. It hurts, though.

Midlife brings home the awareness of this need 'to be the best', the search for perfection mentioned earlier. Neil is coming to terms with it and a more realistic awareness of his abilities.

We don't talk about it very much I guess but there is a sense amongst many of my colleagues that they have compromised with their work. They rely for excellence – that's not the right word – but for whatever I mean by that they rely on the relationships with their wives, mistresses or whatever. They actually rely more on the personal things, those strong emotional things and say almost 'Well screw the work, you'll get by.' You get to the kind of age where you think, 'Well, what the hell, why bust a gut? I'm never going to be the greatest thing in the whole world. I'm good at what I do. I've got some professional skills which I can exercise. I can earn a crust doing that. Do I really want to make a million pounds?'

Compromise need not mean selling out or a soft option. It is also acceptance, resignation, reconciliation, a necessary adjustment. He maps out his own personal requirements.

So long as we have enough to go away twice a year to Cyprus or Greece or deepest France, so long as we have enough to travel around here and see friends, so long as we have enough to make sure our parents don't die in poverty or in abject circumstances, what else do you need? You don't need millions. That's the level of our compromise; it's good, comfy middle-class compromise. We worked for it. I used to wear my social heart on my sleeve. I don't quite so much anymore I guess. I still work for Amnesty. I do those kind of things, which are time consuming. I work on my craft union and their Executive Council so I give back something which I guess is important really.

He recognizes now where he can best direct his energy.

What I can best do is write about political-type issues. Even in television, even in an episode of a pop show, it is possible to look at an extremely human condition and actually make some premise about it. I once showed a scene that we filmed in Belsen between a racist father, his soldier son and a Chinese wife where he talked about 'Jews' and 'niggers' in those terms and he couldn't understand why his Chinese daughter-in-law said 'Are you including me in that – what are you talking about?' It was the strongest thing I've ever written about racism and about what started it. To put that into a standard popular drama on television, I thought, made the point. So at that kind of level I will go on working – and hence become less involved in committee meetings and smokey rooms.

Significant changes have taken place in their family life. In addition to their eldest son, aged eighteen, leaving home, their daughter is about to change school and now the parents are contemplating moving house. It's part of adjusting to the post-parental years to come.

So suddenly, freedom – whoopee! This time next year I'll be free, be off, yeah.

However their freedom of movement is constrained to some extent by the need to consider elderly parents, both sets of whom are still alive. It marks the stage in life, common to many midlife couples, when the relationship with parents becomes 'strong on frustration, weak on gratification'.

My wife's mother is in a home because she couldn't look after her house any more and my parents refused to contemplate old age at the ages of eighty and seventy-eight or whatever. Their lives are very narrow really. They've kind of stayed where they were. They've been happy where they were but you suddenly realize that the number of friends they've kept are very thin on the ground and the whole of their lives are actually lived through their grandchildren, who are down here. I was the only child which makes it more difficult. I mean, I have to be fairly brutally honest about it. I don't want them to come and live with me. I don't think it's fair to them. I'm sure it's not fair to us. Moving them away from the Midlands where they live, to London, or to anywhere else, would be cruel really. It just wouldn't work, and they wouldn't want it. I mean, there's no way they'd want it, but I can see a time coming when one of them dies, and then it's going to be tricky, very difficult.

We promised ourselves all sorts of things when we had the children, about how we would lead our lives after they had left home. God, that's the most exciting bit of it. It's wonderful. I mean the fact that we can think about going to China for a month, and finding the guy who heard your play and wrote to you from Beijing, that would be nice. He heard it at a Radio Festival somewhere, and he did have the courtesy to write and say he liked it and that he'd never not talk to his wife again when he came in from work, so it was sweet. I mean, that kind of adventure. For us it's travel, it's being free to move.

It's the beginning of a new phase in their marriage relationship for them in which then will get to know each other anew.

It was my wife's fiftieth birthday on Wednesday and we drove down to the New Forest. We had a picnic, almost like Darby and Joan, ridiculous really I'm just laughing sitting there in the sunshine. And it was lovely, a great day, a super day. It was a beginning and that was important. One of those days that one will remember I think as the start of something.

But he acknowledges he goes in for volatile mood swings in his working life, characteristic of the swirl of midlife.

Yesterday I was feeling at my bleakest for a very long time in that I'd finished one major piece of work for radio which was an adaptation of a book I wanted to do. Radio actually does these things properly and they cast them right, you know. They don't pay a fortune but you know they'll do it. So that was finished. Then yesterday I'd heard a film I'd written for the BBC was in trouble with the lawyers and we thought it was going to get a 'No'. The lawyers were likely to say 'You can't do it'. It would have been a major breakthrough, because it would have shifted me out of one league into a different kind of league which at forty-seven was make or break. And yesterday there was still no news. I'd got no work. I was thinking about which was the best way to jump off the building – no, that's not true – but I was actually battering my head working on about fifteen different plots and I knew I was getting nowhere but you have to do it and you have to get very tired.

He talks of creative blocks in his life.

I find that when I'm not working, I don't take exercise. When I'm working I swim three times a week. When I'm not working, I stop. I go to sleep in the afternoons. I'm lethargic. I drink too much. It all falls to bits and I guess if you've been doing it for twenty years, and driving yourself for twenty years, because nobody else drives you, when it stops, every so often when it does, you can't handle it. It's very, very hard to handle it. It is the only time I experience fear and it's the fear of not being able to actually come up with another idea, and that scares the shit out of me. I have been six months, nine months without work a couple of times and it's dreadful. It really is very, very frightening. As you get older, you don't bounce. The ideas don't flow in the same way that they used to do. I'm very prolific. I've always got to do something. I have twenty-six ideas out in various shapes: scripts, just notes, or whatever, all out. If they all came together and everyone said 'Yes' I'd be in real trouble. But they do get harder to find. You just slow up. Your mind isn't capable of racing quite so fast.

His solution to the threat of writer's block is to keep going, keep his options open.

It gets harder and I read six books at a time and it's silly. You never know what comes out of all those ideas. I suddenly found one of the ideas I had developed ages and ages ago and realized if I put it with another idea I had, which was totally different, the plot of one and the characters of the other actually worked. Bringing together two opposites, and there is a very good play there. I mean, I have these files full of ideas all over the place. I keep everything, bit of a hoarder actually. I don't have a filing system but I have to keep everything. I actually find I'm now going back and looking at stuff which I wrote six years ago, ten years ago. There's something nice there. I can bring to that the skills I have learnt and I have to do something with it. And that's fun and that's satisfying and you feel you're getting something for nothing.

Through his endeavours and keeping at it, he notices the changes in his work.

The work I'm doing there is getting more complex and more daring. I would never have done it ten years ago. Really getting hold of things. There are ways of using radio which, because you can get inside somebody's head, you can shift time and space in very interesting ways. You can play games with time and you can play games with events in that time which isn't real time but which affects perceptions of the character with regard to whatever else is going on. What enabled me to be bolder? I suppose I just got more confident. I know I'm good. Half is a result of the experience with the health education plays because the public response to those was enormous, just colossal. They ran phone lines to the station, and trailed the programmes very heavily and had experts on then and for a week afterwards. The help lines were open and they had 6,500 calls in a week. I did a play about an alcoholic middle-class lady, almost all of it played inside her head. She was coping with the loss of her children. You work out your own story on these things too. She was coping with children going away, which I knew about because I was partly coping with it myself, so that was fine, but I didn't know about being an alcoholic. Not a lot about it anyway. I've been close in my time but not down the track, and we had the same number of phone calls for that play and that really did surprise me.

He is reaching an awareness of his own ability, and of where his strengths lie.

I think there's a sense that you suddenly realize that you are very powerful. You can do very powerful things. You can actually move people enough to make them pick up a telephone and say 'I want some help – please help me' and that's very salutary in a sense but it's also bloody rewarding. You know you can really turn it on, and, I mean, those plays were both nominations for the Prix d'Italia. They got that kind of kudos too, so there was a kind of big feed-back and producers in other countries asked me to write plays for them and stuff like that. It's great. I mean it's lovely. It's like being patted on the head and told you're good, really. It doesn't much happen in later life does it? You're expected to know you're good or people assume you're alright, but everybody needs a pat on the head.

At midlife this 'need to be needed' is forcefully present. Thinking of the future he has no plans to stop writing.

I think writing is different, writing is a different game really. I mean, I'm not going to retire, with cerebral activity you don't retire from it. It's there and you can't stop it. I mean it's probably quite dangerous but that's life. You know, I'll always write somewhere.

I've had my measure of luck, but not on a plate. You work and you make sure you're in the right place at the right time. And then you make sure you can do it, because if you don't do it that first time, there's no second chance. That's the real killer. It's very hard to get a second shot, particularly in television.

If I can hang on another ten years until I'm fifty-seven I might go away and write my plays for radio, we'd live probably closer to Bath or Bristol, somewhere there is theatre and music and all that. I'm not sure. It's a very dangerous period isn't it? I mean, making a move of this sort is a very dangerous thing to do, to get it right. And you could be stuck in a groove with people you can't stand and there's no way of knowing that until you actually make the jump.

Asked to reflect back on the topic of midlife, he says

I think the key things really were getting used to the kids going away and being given a sense of freedom. Will they stand on their own two feet? I fear for them in this bloody awful world at one level, but it's joy for them in the sense that they're out in the big wide world and it's bloody exciting. It might be scary. The kids moving creates all those waves and all those waves hit you one after the other or one on top of each other, so I think that was the key thing. The sense of failure, the sense of not having achieved what you meant to achieve also lingers around. A play at the National would have been nice. Something with the RSC would be good, something in the theatre would be nice because I've never worked in the theatre. I've worked in all the other media so that would be a kind of just fun thing to do. I might do that.

He's still moving on, still part of his journey.

Body changes are often an early warning system to future difficulties ahead. Being in their way a premonition of eventual death, they are earnestly fought against. The classic midlife symptom is backache, a sign that the support system is beginning to give way and that repressed parts of the self are clamouring to be heard. For those whose work is essentially physical, such as sportsmen or, as in the next story, a ballet dancer, an awareness of what the body is 'saying' is a crucial factor in allowing them to make adjustments in advance, and forestalling the saddest sight of all, a top-notcher past his prime trying to hold on. Timing your exits from one career and building another in anticipation is an important midlife task. Get out while you're on top is the message for footballers who become player-managers, jockeys who become trainers or athletes who become sports coaches. Charles Blyth sensed this and took appropriate action.

Charles Blyth at forty-two is an example of successful adjustment to the demands and pressures of midlife. As a ballet dancer, he knew he had only a limited span of time for his active career. He needed to anticipate the future and change direction in time which he has done by becoming a choreographer. His crisis, or crunch as he calls it, came in his mid thirties. For most ballet dancers this is a critical time as their physical prowess begins to diminish though they still feel able and competent to go on. Being so dependent on physical abilities makes for a high level of tension. He has overcome the physical barrier by converting into a more age-appropriate activity like choreography.

My crisis was not as great as for many people who when they lose their performing ability, often have nothing left and it's a very big crisis to them. For me it was less so because there was a much more even transition. Actually I was looking forward to being forty because then I'd have an excuse to be less good physically as a dancer. Any degeneration would be more acceptable because by his forties a dancer is at the end of his career. It just happens that I've gone into choreography so that my career can continue. I was already much more interested in choreography anyway, even if it's part of that vanity for a dancer who feels the wish still to go to a studio and demonstrate.

I train every day. A lot of choreographers don't bother to train. The nature of my work is very physical and I need to move. Dancers tend to stay psychologically young. They remain almost children and very isolated. The toughness of the profession is such they don't have enough energy and time to do other things. They go home and do their washing and try and relax again and that's it. It's terribly hard. They could be my children whom I'm working with. I had a family outside of it and I had a very 'other world' existence which always kept my feet very firmly on the ground. So I'm not typical of people within my profession.

This 'other world' has been important to him both professionally and in a personal sense.

I feel that I'm much more content with my own company now, I don't worry so much professionally. I've been very fortunate and even when I was being successful and fortunate in the past, I still used to be very insecure and worry a lot. Now I don't and when I come away from work I don't think about my work. I don't have sleepless nights anymore. I almost turn off in the studio and I really enjoy work; I enjoy the working process. My energy keeps going longer and if I have a failure, it doesn't mean so much. I'm much more philosophical about not doing well.

Taking on the challenge of the transition to choreographer at midlife has enabled him to become more relaxed and philosophical about his work. Instead of living out the pressures of work as many of his contemporaries do, he diffuses them in his family life, which has gained in importance.

In the last seven or eight years I have put a determined effort into giving my family more time. I suddenly realized that I hadn't given enough time to my children. I have been very much enjoying the time I spend with my wife. The fact that we've now bought this house in Somerset is wonderful, it's like a paradise for us and it's like a step on to another life. I'm now in a position where I can work and choose my free time when I want to but it has taken until recently to get to that position. I feel almost like I'm in semi-retirement but my retirement is a very physical one because I'm being creative in the country and in the garden we have there, which I'm getting more and more fascinated with and that has partly taken the place of my work.

Nevertheless giving up dancing was quite a wrench.

There's no experience quite like giving a performance, giving a good performance and coming out on the stage and have the audience applauding you. It gets the adrenalin really flowing, like with actors and sportsmen in football and cricket – you're achieving something. Being a dancer was physically taxing. You had a good sweat as well as anything else and the nature of the roles that I did, I did some dramatic things, made it a real experience; it was a piece of theatre; a piece of dance. The beauty of that drink, that beer at the end of the show. Beer has never tasted the same since I stopped performing. I felt like Superman sometimes; you have a certain power or magic you control and I know as a performer that one of my strengths is that I had a lot of magnetism as a performer and I could feel that holding an audience. You feel like a god, I did anyway. You feel totally in control and you have power in your hands but of course it's very much ego and vanity.

I've got over the crisis of not performing any more. At times I miss the chance to actually act but I really don't want to get into that anymore anyway. I enjoy the luxury of my position of making others do it. That's one of the nice things about choreography, I think, not having to worry too much: not worrying about being physically so attractive; not worrying so much about how you look or what impression you're making. You're not bothered about that any more and you can smile when you see younger people self-conscious and trying to make that effort. Now as a choreographer it's all over a longer period of time and once I've done a ballet and got it on, there's almost sadness because it's like giving birth to something and it takes so long and it's actually an independent part of me.

He has thought of other routes to take as an extension of his career.

I don't think I'd now go along the acting performing route, not unless a remarkable opportunity came up. I'd do it occasionally, but I'm not going back to square one to train and learn the techniques. Working with the RSC over the last month, the amount of good actors that actually didn't have a good basic training and came from all other types of backgrounds, is quite amazing. Often it's the ones with the more 'stagey' performance that have had the training and the more vital and more exciting ones haven't had the training. They've picked it up as they go along. You learn it through speaking and practice and I must say working with the RSC I love the idea of performing. As you get older in dance you get so little to do in terms of mime role. Having had wonderful things to dance, the opportunity to do mime roles is interesting.

But in his switchover at midlife he's looking to the dimensions of his life outside his field of work as much as those in it. He feels he has 'reached a stage where that energy is freed'. But he also notes that he has been

. . . waiting for a long time to actually develop a wisdom with the advancing years and it seemed to come terribly slowly. As you look back you realize how naive you were for so long and just how your whole attitude to life totally changes and you can see how older people look – obviously they had that wisdom earlier but there was no way they could actually explain it to you, just as there is now way you can really explain it to your children and younger people.

As part of his midlife 'getting of wisdom' he looks back over his life and reflects on things that he might have wished to have done differently.

A lot of things I couldn't actually alter. I wish I hadn't been quite so intensive about my career. I wish I had had the ability to shut off more and had the courage to risk my career by involving myself more in my family, I do regret that very much. I regret the time when I knew my father was ill in hospital and I didn't just 'down tools' and go up there. I stayed because there were important rehearsals that I didn't want to miss and my mother in a sense reassured me that he was going to be alright and I said I would try and get up at the week-end and I should have gone because the police knocked at the door several days later and he was dead and I know he was asking after me. Having my own children now, I know what it would have meant to have seen me. I should have been there and in a sense I've never forgiven myself for that and it was a kind of selfishness that I think I have been guilty of quite often. In some respects I've had to be quite selfish otherwise I wouldn't have had the career that I have but there were times when it was totally unnecessary for me to sort of dedicate myself so entirely to my career.

Midlife also brings doubts about the value and worth of his creative abilities. For all his success, each new venture represents an anxious-making fresh start, just as the most experienced actors never get over first night nerves.

I fluctuate between being very confident, on top of the tree of success and one of only a handful of choreographers in the world that have an international career, whose pieces are wanted. There is work to keep me busy for years. On the other hand, I am very critical of my own work and see it, not subjectively, but objectively, I am critical of it not being good enough and I worry that people are going to actually see it when the work isn't as good as I thought it was. I think if you can create maybe three masterpieces that actually can be re-created again and again and can live and stand the test of time, then you have done very well as a choreographer. I've done a couple that have stood that test of time. Once it's gone on stage I feel it's out of my hand. I actually can't sit through my own ballets, very rarely. I hate going out there with an audience. I feel very vulnerable. I think if it lives in people's memories that's important.

I hope to leave a body of work, by then probably a small body of work, because a lot will be forgotten. I'm working with kids and a company that never really knew me as a dancer. They hear about my performances some of them but there was a time when I knew that I had such a reputation – you would be held in awe. Now, they couldn't care less, they really don't know who I am. The name may ring a bell with some young kids of fifteen or sixteen. They know me as a choreographer some of them, if they are in tune at all, but as a dancer I'm not known anymore. Ok there are two films of me doing two roles and those must have been seen but it's the reputation in books, magazines. They just don't read all that anymore.

He finds a ready outlet for much of his creativity on his country house now.

I have always enjoyed being creative. I like to get lost in physical, manual labour too, and especially if at the end of it you have created something, like a nice wall or a beautifully dug patch of soil, rich, damp earth and to see vegetables and flowers coming up. It's very exciting, I love that, I'm a child in that respect. I like physical hard labour out of doors, I love it. I hope that I can maintain physical fitness that will enable me to do a lot in the garden because I dread the day when it's all finished. Maybe when it's done, I'll turn to making things, as I love working wood. I haven't really done it for so many years. And reading, I love having more time to read, to get back to the books I'm reading now. When I get back to working with my hands, I feel as if I'm getting closer towards my wife's area of work as an artist. I love the idea of us being able to work side by side on our individual things because she's got very interested in making constructions now and working in wood and the result is that we are coming together and I help her with the woodwork and then she's helping me.

Blyth was fortunate to anticipate the changeover in his life. Timing in his case was crucial. For Dennis Churston, the pressure of events had begun to build up to such an extent that he felt he was in danger of losing his creative side altogether.

Dennis Churston, now fifty-one years old, is a composer and pianist who runs the music department at a College of Further Education. His personal crisis came just over ten years ago in his late thirties when he felt he was going downhill, slipping into a way of life that had little meaning for him. 'I think it's easy to get into, you start to earn enough money to be comfortable and to be able to enjoy some of the material things.' But this emphasis on materialism, in itself part of the consolidation of adult achievement, meant a sort of death of the soul. 'It can easily take over and you start just being social and not being discriminating about who you see and what you do.' Easy as it was to fall into the trap, he soon saw himself as 'just going to work and doing one's job and not doing anything more than that with one's life.' Admittedly he was under pressure from work, the strain of running a department in the climate of public spending cuts made itself felt. He knew his creative side was going to waste and recognizes that he 'could easily have given up', not because he 'didn't have any more to say' but pressures at work were taking up so much of his time and home life was spent recuperating from work pressures. This covered a span of some five years, and in its way may have been a necessary preliminary to his later more productive years.

Then, at the age of forty, he realized that if he was to have any self-respect, he had to 'go on doing his composing and playing', and express more of his creative side. Performing in public provided a necessary boost to his self-esteem, 'getting up in front of an audience and having them clapping'. Defensively, he recognizes this as something of an ego trip, a necessary one nevertheless, as though he needed to nourish his underused talent. At middle age, such mirroring back of approval as an audience clapping enhances a shaky sense of self-worth. He was suddenly, pressingly aware of the shortage of time, as if he'd been seduced by the lure of materialism and had forsaken what he knew was fundamentally important to him and what ultimately gave him more satisfaction than anything else. 'I'd started to be more creative . . . if you have this need, I think you've got to do it, otherwise you're miserable, you're in agony.' But it meant sacrifices at a point in life when many are tempted to put their feet up.

It was bloody hard work doing a full-time job, then coming home in the evenings and working, especially at week-ends when everybody else was having fun, going out to exhibitions and things like that, going out to dinner parties. Not that I didn't go out to dinner parties, but I knew I had to get my head down and work at times when perhaps a lot of people would want to be free to relax. The end result is that you get stressed, that's a middle age phenomenon, I think.

Having had the five year moratorium, he found he was able to move ahead from producing his 'early stuff which was trying to conform to the establishment' and composing instead 'the things I have wanted to write and not the things that I think I ought to be writing, less conscious of fashion and what the leading figures are doing.' He was finding his own authentic voice. He started up yoga and autogenic training partly to relieve the stress he was under and partly to capitalize on his new-found sense of energy. Time and the proper use of it have acquired special significance for him. 'I get very covetous of my time, more and more.'

The revival of his creative activity paid off in other directions. He was promoted to Head of Department at about the same time. His personal life also moved forward. He and his partner, Stephen, who had lived together for over twenty years, decided finally to buy a house for the first time rather than continue living in flats, bringing more permanence and solidity to their lives. Dennis relishes the notion of home. 'I feel quite deprived if I don't have an hour sitting down in the evening with a book and a drink when I get in.'

He seems now to have got his creative and working life in balance together. The fact that he has only a limited amount of time for his creative side doesn't worry him.

I think it's very interesting to have a limit to the amount of time and see what you can do with it. It's amazing what you can get done. I know that when I have all day, as during the vacation, I waste sometimes four-fifths of it. I get really good work done in a very short space of time, so it is possible to do a lot of useful work in addition to one's support job.

He feels 'tremendous responsibility towards my students, making sure they are getting what they need, what they want, the right course, the right kind of teaching, the right balance of things.' It's an 'intense relationship. I try to be generous and giving with my students particularly. I try to have a very good relationship with them. I think I'm probably very conscious that it does compensate for family things.' Such a relationship allows him to express parental-type feelings towards them, and alleviates some of the guilt he feels.

'One feels very guilty about not having had to bear the responsibility of having children and selfish in a way. I look at friends who are married with children, and I realize what an easy time I have and that I opted out of certain responsibilities there.' Guilt is a word that crops up every so often in his conversation. He talks of his feelings of guilt more openly now perhaps as a result of the climate of acceptance of his being gay has changed. This has to some extent been paralleled by the shift in direction in his own life.

Nevertheless he is still sensitive to the transient nature of happiness, its precariousness. 'I sometimes feel that when one is particularly comfortable and happy, it can easily be taken away, superstitious in a way.'

A constant thread through all these stories is the importance of allowing change to take place, of allowing the 'drift, wait and obey' of Kipling's quote to happen, of allowing other voices to permeate a person's life temporarily, and undeveloped sides to have their say. Midlife is a time of flux, of change in the Heraclitean sense: you never cross the same river twice. It is a question of giving up as much as holding on. Hemingway felt intense despair in the later part of his writing career: 'It won't come anymore.' In some sense he was trying to repeat the same formula. Yet at other times he let his unconscious remain open to source material, to his 'Daemon'. On a fishing trip from Cuba, he passed a small fishing boat on his way back with an old man and a boy in it. He had called across to them asking if they wanted help. The old man swore and cursed him roundly for interfering. 'Leave me alone.' But years later this was to be the origin for his prize-winning novel, *The Old Man and the Sea*.

Borges called writing a 'guided dream', a recognition of the interplay of conscious and unconscious forces. Every creative act requires its own process. There are stages to go through – of preparation, of sifting, of waiting, of testing. Unless these are 'allowed' to happen, a tensing-up is likely to occur instead. Bertrand Russell discovered this when he first started writing. 'Each fresh piece of serious work used to seem to me for a time – perhaps a long time – to be beyond my powers. I would fret myself into a nervous state from fear that it was never going to come right. I would make one unsatisfying attempt after another, and in the end have to discard them all.' After a while he found that such 'fumbling attempts' were a waste of time. What he needed was a 'period of subconscious incubation which could not be hurried and was, if anything, impeded by deliberate thinking.' Sometimes he would find that he had to cancel the book he was thinking of writing, but often this incubation period produced results. 'Having, by the time of very intense concentration, planted the problem in my sub-consciousness, it would germinate underground until, suddenly, the solution emerged with blinding clarity, so that it only remained to write down what had appeared as if in revelation.'

Painters recognize the value of letting go, letting the unconscious do its work. Paul Klee spoke of taking a line for walk, and Picasso, exploring his inner world on canvas, boldly asserted '*Je ne cherche pas, je trouve*'.

The crunch at midlife often comes over the question of the search for perfection, of being good enough, the feeling that only the best will do. It is linked to the notion of upwards progress, that all is heading towards some future goal of perfect achievement, a limitless existence. To aim for less is not to become second-rate. It's getting to understand better where one's real abilities and talents lie, a source of potential strength. This is a move away from the fear of failure and reliance on an already fragile self-esteem. Accepting that there are limits to one's ability is accepting that there are limits elsewhere, that one is mortal after all. Accepting both these factors needn't be catastrophic. They can be lived with and ultimately made use of. Jaques wrote in his paper 'Death and the Midlife Crisis': 'One's work need no longer be perfect. It can be worked and reworked, but it will be accepted as having shortcomings . . . There is no need for obsessional attempts at perfection, because inevitable imperfection is no longer felt as bitter persecuting failure. Out of this mature resignation comes serenity which transcends imperfection by accepting it.' The mature resignation, far from being passive, can be the motivator for more reflective work. Dante writing the *Divine Comedy* is a case in point, the classic example of a writer working through the 'depressive crisis' of midlife via his writing. In describing his journey through his past via the descending circles of hell, accompanied by Virgil who stands both for tradition and the masculine principle, and then on through purgatory to paradise (helped now by Beatrice, representative of his feminine side) Dante accepts the errors of his past, learns to mourn it and the guilt and anxiety involved, before recognizing the necessity of death and the supreme importance and understanding of God who unifies heaven and earth.

It is a final act of reconciliation, of making peace with oneself and with the world.

Everyone carries this creative ability within themselves, though most of us lose it on the way. Freud once wrote: 'The creative writer does the same as the child at play, he creates a world of fantasy which he takes very seriously. As people grow up they cease to play and they seem to give up the yield of pleasure which they gain from playing.' Midlife offers the chance to get in touch again with this ability to play, to experiment, to try things out. Let Freud have the last word: 'Get it out, produce it, make something of it – outside you, that is; give it an existence independent of you.'

9

Escape

No man is an island entire of itself

JOHN DONNE

The best-known example of midlife escape is that of Gauguin. Quitting his bank job in Paris aged thirty-three, he fled eventually to Tahiti in search of primitive simplicity in exotic surroundings. Distancing himself as much as he could from the world he had known, it is hardly surprising that sooner or later his 'past' and his European inheritance caught up with him. His pictures begin to capture this mood of doubt. His Tahitian Holy Family attempts to create a merger of the two cultures but they sit awkwardly side by side. The paintings of brooding, recumbent Tahitian women indicate how inaccessible their inner life was to the painter. For all his wish to immerse himself in their life, Gauguin could not shed his otherness. It was always there inside him. In desperation he decided to kill himself in 1897 aged forty. Before doing so he completed, feverishly, his last great testamentary picture and wrote on it, as a form of signature, the great midlife cry – 'Where have we come from? What are we? Where are we going?' Then Gauguin took his arsenic but the dose was too large, he vomited and lived. Life had triumphed, 'surged up' as he wrote when describing this picture: 'I put into it all my energy, a passion so painful in terrible circumstances and a vision so clear, that life surges up.'

Midlife is often the springboard for a complete change of lifestyle: a city businessman buying a farm, an accountant running a guest house are example of moves designed to launch a second career in changed surroundings. It's partly the search for renewal, for rejuvenation even. For some trapped in the city, dreams of escape, of fleeing the urban nightmare, begin to surface accompanied by images of the good life, of a nostalgic return to nature. The urge to retreat, to discover self-sufficiency is nowadays sharpened by anxieties about the destruction of the environment and of the ecological damage being done to the planet.

In the case of Terence Crossley both of these contributed to his decision to leave London and move to rural Wales. He's thirty-eight and blind, and has been living in central Wales with his wife and four children for just under a year. Before, he worked as a civil servant in the Department of Education in London but wanted to 'quit while I was ahead'. Now he's relishing the novelty of it. 'I keep having to pinch myself to remind myself that I am not merely on a long holiday.'

Their pebbled-dashed house, set in a small valley, lies beyond Carmarthen. It's cosy inside, all bright and clean, a fresh start for them all. Children and animals are everywhere – goats, cats, an Alsatian dog and 'four children roaring about the place like a gaggle of mini-whirlwinds' as Terence warns visitors. He is a dark, heavy Celtic man with a huge black beard, the sort of man who has presence. He senses the proffered hand and shakes it warmly. Dressed informally, in yellow T-shirt, with cords and trainers, he moves slowly and a bit heavily.

Wales is a return to his Celtic past for him. He gets up early on Saturdays to listen to Celtic songs on the radio. The peacefulness of his valley is briefly shattered by low-flying fighter planes on radar-avoidance exercises, 'the price of a new hospital roaring overhead at an alarmingly low altitude' as Terence comments. Having fled to the countryside to get away from all that, it's ironical to find it catching up with him. He's alarmed about the state of the world ('We'll all be blown out of existence by five years time') and acknowledges that perhaps the main reason for his shift to the countryside is to secure the future safety of his children.

Perhaps plan would be too strong a word to describe the changes in my life. For many years the idea of leaving London cropped up and was tossed away. We had a good friend called Kevin with whom we'd talk about going to Donegal and another friend, a Scot, to pore over maps of the North West with. Then last year the real possibility of a move came up again because of the way house prices had taken off in our part of London. Ann (his wife) came down here at the beginning of August with a sheaf of possibilities and found this place and we had moved by October.

Neither of us knew Wales really. We just grabbed the thing by the horns. It may sound a brave thing to do but it would take a brave man to spend another thirty years on the treadmill, or stay in the Department of Education (where he'd worked since 1974) the way things were going.

His mother, a young-looking seventy-four, came to join them.

I've put myself back in the bosom of the family. We're a close family anyway but I was spending the major part of my working life away from them, especially the young twin girls (aged five). There's a kind of safety in coming here. There's mother there, I suppose that's a secure thing. We're in an area where I hope the children will feel much more secure and I feel much more secure for them. We've adopted a different way of life, time to lean on the gate and talk to someone or go and have a beer. I go running on Wednesday afternoon when I would have been slaving at work.

We live on our ill-gotten gains from the house price. Well, I'm a Government artist as well, so I draw the dole. Also my mother has put money into the house which has freed some of the profits that we made. So, we've joined the idle rich. I tell people we're into alternative lifestyles but we happen to like eating pulses. I'll eat meat, Ann's essentially a vegetarian, but I'll eat meat if it comes my way. I was paying £500 a month for the mortgage and £60 a month on rates, £40 or £50 on travel and had a couple of pounds in my pocket each day to buy a cup of coffee and lunch, so really the best part of £700 was expended on simply being in a position to go to work each day. Here we don't have a mortgage and the rates are £180 a year.

We spend £25 or £30 a month on milk but once the goats are on stream, that will stop. Chickens provide us with eggs; we sell a few which just about pays for the price of their corn. So we have free eggs and free milk and we've planted a load of spuds and other vegetables and fruit trees. So the expenses are so much smaller, and we can still afford to buy a book or record. Neither of us are great for going out to restaurants or flicks, or whatever, so we don't miss that you know.

He compares his life now with his previous London life.

I was talking to a former colleague only today who made envious noises, and my response is 'Well, do it, if you can afford it' but she felt that money wasn't actually the main consideration, there was a degree of fear attached to it. I can understand that of course, but I haven't yet once woken up in the night thinking 'Is this the right thing?' Maybe because Ann was so wholeheartedly in favour of it and my mother was, and the kids seemed to be. There was nobody nagging round the edge of one's mind sowing seeds of doubt.

He considers what he misses about London.

There's an old Welsh poet who asks God why he made the world so beautiful and his life so short. I think I can understand what he means. You know, why spend it in a concrete jungle, the old cliché, stuck in the middle of London, six storeys up listening to police sirens, dreadful. I miss the skiff and punt racing. We used to live on the river and I did a lot of it. I've joined the longboat club over the estuary, so I'm going rowing now. Once the sea gets warmer, I hope to do some canoeing there, so that side of things is being looked after. We miss one or two friends, but in a strange way probably we will see more of them down here, or get bigger doses less often. Quite a few of my closest friends by accident of career or whatever have moved to other parts of the country, so I didn't see them as often as I would have liked. There's a handful in London who I will continue to see. The guy I used to race with has been down here already for a while and we've been out on the water here, so I think it's just the skiffing and the punting.

I came down here full of plans. I mean one project that I want to do is write a book on the dialect songs of the British gypsies and tinkers, the traditional songs. I've collected notes for a long time and texts but I've looked at them only once. Time just absolutely flies by. I haven't read a book since I've been down here; the only intellectual stimulation I've had is reading up Welsh. Perhaps it's one of those things: journeying is better than arriving. If you actually finish it, you deflate like a punctured balloon.

I've never really had wide horizons. I don't think it's really necessary to think about five years time, ten years time. We'll all be blown out of existence by then. There's not a lot of point. I don't mean by that that it is something that is constantly in my mind, but there just does not seem to me to be any point in contemplating a long-term future. When we were living in London we were always grossly under-insured by any normal standards but Ann used to say 'What's the point?' and I suppose I agree with her really. You live life, it's short enough anyway without thinking too much about what's going to happen. It's no good blinding yourself from the fact that we're all going down the same path or certain changes are going to happen as you get older. The children will leave home and so on and so forth. One of us will die before the other, probably, but I don't think there's anything in my make-up that makes me want to plan for it. If it will happen, it will happen.

I think physically and emotionally I would say that I'm much more like my father. He died of cancer at the age of sixty. He'd not come from a very long-lived family, so maybe I'll go out in my sixties, I don't know, but again, why worry about that? I like to think, like Socrates, when death isn't there I am and when it is I'm not. Death doesn't frighten me one iota. Dying does but death doesn't, no. I mean, I look at the options and I think 'Ok if there's this benign deity that people talk about, I shouldn't be too badly off – I've been a bit of skunk occasionally – but I'm no crook. If there isn't, you know, good-night, put out the light.' Ok there's always that possibility that it's all a monstrous trick of some evil design and that once we die . . . but you're getting into the realms of total speculation there.

I mean life's important, yes, we're here, and that's what you've got to think about. You know we're all dealt a different hand, aren't we? We don't start off with the same advantages or disadvantages. Certainly a bit unfortunate if we're all judged by some yardstick. Just can't worry about it.

These thoughts plus his blindness give him an impetus to make the most of his time.

I was born totally blind, and I got sight back, whilst I was still a babe in arms. My parents were told that I would lose sight in my late teens. As a very young boy I remember hankering after the countryside. I used to find at my first school that by the end of the day I was almost gasping to get out into the air. It was a physical thing, you'd look through the window and you'd see these amazing colours, autumn or whatever, and then the back of the wall. This is no way to spend life, I thought. The romantic in me always thought it would be great to go off with the tinkers. I was kicked in the eye playing football when I was about eleven or twelve and that put paid to one eye, but it would have gone anyway. It got to the point where I couldn't see to read. I went on to Worcester College for the Blind. I was about half way through 'A' levels when I transferred into Braille. It was a slow and rather painful process which probably finished when I was about twenty when I couldn't see to get about either. By about twenty-one, my sight had gone. I spent about a year without anything because I just couldn't bear the idea of a stick or anything like that because it seemed to me like shutting the door, acknowledging a fact which I didn't want to acknowledge. I think those couple of years were very difficult. I felt it was an emasculation, the worst thing was the feeling of abject humiliation. Not exactly that it was my fault, but if you walk into something or whatever, you know, 'God I'm an idiot' whereas in fact it's a logical progression. Also I suppose at that age, you're very much conscious of yourself and how you appear to the opposite sex. Blindness is a bit of a problem when you want to swing through the trees beating your chest. I was a bit edgy. I can remember one girl I did know at college saying to me 'Why do you have to be such a bastard all the time?' She was a good friend, actually. It was a good thing she said that, as I think what I did was an effort to make sure that what I received was not pity, I would give it out before I got it. You know, it's pretty much standard stuff, standard routine I think, so it wasn't too clever a time in many ways, but, as I said to you, life goes on.

I'm not for one moment suggesting I was anywhere near cracking up under the strain. I couldn't because there were so many people around me doing so many things, and I mean I was a bit of misery, but you know, I suppose life looked a bit tasty, so I thought 'Well, get on with it'.

It's daft the things that really screw you up at certain times. I think probably the first time I was out with a girl and I had to say to her 'Can you show me where the toilet is please?' was one of them. God, it's something that you wouldn't give a thought about now; if you wanted to go and relieve yourself, you're not too worried what people think, all you're doing is asking to be shown to a door, but to do that when you're in your first flush of manhood, it's that sort of thing that's hard. Women in the main don't have the same ghastly hang-ups as men anyway and usually find it easier to handle that kind of thing, or to handle physical impairment, than men do.

Ann and he are

. . . alike in many ways. We react in the same way and have the same outlook on life. We can sit in the house, she can sit in one room and I can sit in another, and we don't need to sit on top of each other. Neither of us on a daily basis needs too much conversation. I'm quite happy pottering about outside doing something and she's inside pottering about. Neither of us are great party-goers. We don't like crowds of people. We have broadly the same outlook on things like religion, and planning for the future and whatever.

Thoughts of work, a job, have been shelved for the moment.

They wrote to me and said 'Come and see the Restart Officer,' but I doubt if they're going to be able to find anything for a blind unemployed graduate in a 24 per cent unemployment area, but you never know your luck, or your lack of luck. At the moment I'm still on holiday. I think it's so brilliant. I get up in the morning, don't lie in bed. I get up maybe 6.30 whatever, come down and make the tea and do the boiler and go outside and it's just so amazing. The spring's bubbling away – first crow of the day and I just think it's so fantastic that I haven't done anything yet. In a way I'm still on holiday. Come back in six years time, I might be going up the wall. It's very easy to disengage, and maybe there's a little bit of me, the service ethic bit, that says 'Hey you've got to put something back in – if you get such a kick out of it, you've got to put a bit in'. That hasn't troubled me as yet, but maybe that's something that will begin to happen over time.

He compares himself with his brother.

My brother, he's one of the better educated and better-read scientists that I know, is now in a computer consultancy. He leaves home at 7 or 7.30 and may get home about 8, may stay in London overnight. He'll bring work home. Towards the end of the month, he realizes he's got to play six games of squash to keep up in his squash league so he goes away and does that (he's built like a weevil, God knows how he plays squash). Sometimes he sounds utterly exhausted and I say 'You're mad'. He says 'I envy you'. I say 'Either you're lying or you're mad – one or the other'. He's got a good marriage is very fond of his wife (she's smashing) has three nice kids and a really good set-up (they're a loving family) and I say: 'Why are you doing this to yourself? I really don't understand why you're giving yourself an hour a day with your two older daughters and sometimes not seeing your younger daughter – Why are you doing it?'

Midlife is a question of ordering priorities. If he'd stayed at the DES he could have eased back on work in order to have more time with the family, not aimed for promotion.

I can count on one hand the number of times I took work home. I would knock off and say 'That's it, if I can't do the work in a working day, either I'm not up to it, or it's too much for me, one or the other, the situation is not right.' And if someone said to me 'This has got to be done by 3.30 yesterday, I'd either say 'Yes, I'll do it' or I would say 'No'. Eventually I was slung out of the fast stream. I can remember the interview to this day. He said 'I'm going to give you an A for this and an A for that and A for the other, but I'm only going to recommend you for immediate promotion to the next grade rather than grade skipping because you won't do what the bosses want.' I said 'What do you mean by that?' and he said 'Well if you know that they favour a particular line or they want a particular thing done, you don't always jump to it.' So I said, 'What do you mean – do you mean if I have a different view I shouldn't put it?' I said 'That's not possible.' If having put my view you say 'Well despite that do this' then I'll either do it or resign. And he said 'Well, I agree with you in the pub, but this is the hierarchy.' I can remember I said 'Well, stuff it.' I was going to ruin my career by being forthright. But you know, at that point, I thought to myself 'This is ridiculous.'

Another watershed was when I had to do a submission to Ministers on the reorganization of a particular secondary provision, and they wanted it by whatever time, and I had a woman working for me then who was exceedingly loyal, Dorothy her name was, she lived in Woking. She used to see to her husband and her grandson who lived with her, because the marriage of her daughter had gone wrong. She used to come in from Woking having done all their stuff and stand on the train as often as not, work, do her shopping in the lunch-hour, work and then go back on this train and do her husband's tea and the rest of that stuff. Anyway, she stayed one night till 8 o'clock to type up that work for me, so it could be there on the desk the next morning. It sat on that desk for three weeks and I thought, 'Well you bastards. I'm not playing that game.'

It became a game after that. You start to think, 'How can I go on with this?' A great friend of mine at work, likes wearing hand-painted Japanese ties, so you start off by finding a sports jacket instead of a suit. You're waiting for someone to say something and then in come the T-shirts and by the time I'd finished I was wearing white trousers, jeans, T-shirts, anything, and nobody was saying anything and you'd think 'What are they thinking?' 'Perhaps tomorrow I'll come in stark naked.'

All these factors helped crystallize his decision to move. He says he got 'this awful peep behind the curtains' of the way work was being organized.

He also started working with the Samaritans at about that time. He feels it may have been something to do with his father, who had been a Probation Officer and worked 'all hours God sends'. He had admired him and he had noted the 'immense satisfaction he'd been able to give to people'. Wishing to emulate him in some respect, he became more involved in counselling work, and recalls seeing someone in their mid-thirties with a good marriage and a good family life sitting in the office blubbing his eyes out, because things had just got so far out of control at work. It helped him make up his mind to leave. I thought to myself 'Not for me'. A move to the country, the dream of rural bliss, may, he accepts, have a touch of unreality about it.

Maybe I'm trying to weave a cocoon for myself and live my comfortable dream which is no more reality than being a stockbroker. But this feels right for me. Let them get on with it and let me get on with it. Coming down here represents not simply a flight from or towards, but elements of both. There were elements of my life there that were unsatisfactory and there were possibly things I wished to go towards so it wasn't just a blind rush away.

Within their marriage, his relationship with his wife has changed, as she takes more of a dominant role.

I'm more dependent on Ann. Until last year Ann was doing her stuff at home, very practical. She would mend the washing machine before I got home, or I'd scrape off the outside of the house and she would paint it, she would do most things. But I brought home the bread and so it was a joint contribution. Here the balance has shifted markedly towards Ann. Most things down here she will do better than I will. The only thing she won't do is joinery and I like that. She's probably better at cleaning out chickens than I am because she can see. That occurred to me as a possible problem, not because I'd start feeling useless because I don't think along those lines, but that she would feel overburdened. That hasn't occurred yet, but occasionally she is annoyed that I can't see and I annoy her by saying 'You think it's bad for you that I can't see, what do you think it's like for me?'

The other thing that may mean difficulty, and is still there, is that I never had ambition in the conventional sense. But I suspect it was quite important to me to have achieved a degree of success, so that the unspoken might be 'I'm blind', but the spoken bit would be 'I'm such and such'. That's the yardstick I'd wish to be judged by casual acquaintances. Going back to the idea of not wanting pity, if I could say 'That's my job,' people would take me more seriously. I think that's largely disappeared but when it disappeared I kept wondering if I would feel the need to say, 'Until last October I was . . . and now I do nothing?' There's probably a bit of that occasionally. I get that in, then I kick myself, but it's still there. But as time goes by I imagine it'll change.

Looking back, he realizes he wanted to have his cake and eat it, wanted his music, his books. Now he's got it but there is a momentary anxiety whether it could all fall apart. Ironically, as he says, it is in his interest for the interest rate to go up.

I listen to the radio and hear the rate has gone down and think 'Oh no,' but I should be delighted for everyone else. It's unreal. Also there's a feeling that by coming down here I can endanger the very thing I came for. The mass migration of South-East England to West Wales can corrupt the very fruit we came to nibble at. Bits of land are being sold off around here. I say I don't want them to be but they're only coming for what I came for. There's a local lad near here who wants to buy his own farm, his own house; he'll never get a farm, maybe not a house. I just hope they don't think we're the sort of people who've given newcomers a bad reputation in some areas.

There are, as always, undercurrents of conflicting ideas.

10

Fathers

Le roi est mort, vive le roi.

The death of the father is arguably the most significant event in a man's life. Freud considered this to be the case and was in midlife himself, aged forty, when his father died. He was forcefully reminded of the hostility he had felt towards him while he was alive. As he sought to repair this through his own analysis, his guilt turned into an appreciation of what his father had really stood for and meant to him. It was a period of 'deep-reaching interior transformation'. In this book many interviewees have referred to the death of their father and described this moment with particular feeling.

Philip Raymond is now forty-six years old. Married at the age of nineteen, he was quickly successful as a businessman, setting up some of the first theme parks in the UK. Then his father died when he was in his early thirties. This was a traumatic and formative event for him. He took a crucial decision. He wanted to be sure of having something to pass on to his wife and children, especially his son. The death of his father, bringing home to him the notion of time running out and reminding him he was the next one in line, made him set up his own business, and also, as part of his sense of generational continuity, to begin writing children's stories.

My parents were in the theatre so I was brought up in the theatre and as a young child I travelled quite a lot with them. My mother was forty-three when I was born and my father was forty-nine. I had a sister thirteen years older than me. Looking back in life, I remember getting my father to play football or to give me piggy-backs – he must have been into his mid fifties by then, and I couldn't understand why he shouldn't.

My father was a gentleman. Very, very nice, pleasant, passive sort of man. He had done a lot of amazing things. He had made the first television show in the world for Logie Baird on a six-foot stage. He had been to South Africa during or just after the Zulu uprising. He used to send me to sleep at night telling me stories of the jackals in Africa. He was a very, very interesting man. When he died about twelve or fourteen years ago it was probably one of the worst experiences I've had in my life.

Even though you have parents that are older, you become accustomed to the fact that nothing will ever happen to them. He had been seriously ill on a couple of occasions, once when he'd had a major ulcer and the second time when he had obviously had a recurrence of the ulcer. He got through it, so I thought that he would never ever be vulnerable to death, but he very quickly deteriorated. He was taken into hospital and within three months he was dead. He was a man of about my height, tall, very good-looking man. I was in London and my wife went up to look after him and my mother. When I came up, he had deteriorated to six stone, so I stayed with him. I sent everybody else away and I stayed with him until, eventually, the end. But, I mean, he was the classic gentleman because he could see obviously I was extremely upset. And when he died, he had an oxygen mask on – and when they die, just before they die, they get totally better – and he took the oxygen mask off and sat up in bed and said 'Don't cry.' I felt for some reason or other everything had happened and it was tremendous, and he said, 'Son, look at that boy across there' – a man of about thirty. He said, 'He has a young family and he is someone that needs someone. I've had a good life. I just want you to look after your mother.' He went back down in his bed and died so that was a very traumatic period in my life.

Charles Blyth thinks back to his father's death and the implications this had for him now and then.

I do regret that very much. I regret the time when I knew my father was ill in hospital and I just didn't 'down tools' and just go up there. I stayed because there were important rehearsals that I didn't want to miss and my mother in a sense reassured me that he was going to be alright and I said I would try and get up at the week-end and I should have gone because the police knocked at the door several days later and he was dead and I know he was asking after me. Having my own children now, I know what it would have meant to have seen me. I should have been there and in a sense I've never forgiven myself for that.

The same sort of feeling is shared by Henry King whose father lay dying in a Newcastle Hospital during the winter of 1978 at a time when he was fully

taken up with parliamentary duties and was unable to spare the time to visit him. Now, still thinking about that time, he's coming to recognize how much of his father is in him. It's a way of building bridges back to his father and healing the wounds of his neglect.

I now see more of my relatives, more of my family in me, than I did and more of my father in me, and my mother in me than I have done hitherto. I'm less of a totally independent being, more the child of my parents and my family. I see the ambitious mother in me, occasionally thoughtless and hurtful, as I am to other people occasionally, and I see the kind father.

Neil Marlowe feels he's been living the 'unlived life of the parents' with all the complications that brings. His father would have liked to have been a writer himself.

My father did a job which required a lot of physical labour. He wanted to be a writer, but you couldn't be when you were his age, I mean when he was born. My father comes from a generation and a background where it was almost impossible for him to become one. He feels jealous about my career but never talks about it. Never ever talks about it, never asks how my work's doing. Never wants to read a piece of work. I never offer. He probably listens to Radio 4. But he'll listen to it and tell the neighbours, then the neighbours listen to it . . . and I'm aware of his gathering some kudos from that. Fine. It's no skin off my nose. Still . . . I'm not him. To be brutally honest, he'd never suspected I'd have the tenacity to be a writer. It's not easy to be a writer or any kind of artist really. One forgets it's hard graft. It wasn't handed to me on a plate.

The lack of paternal approval has hurt him but also been a spur to his career as a writer. Having achieved a measure of success, he's now in a position to re-assess where he stands in relation to his father, but it's left an uneasy mixture of resentment and some guilt.
For Barry Hanson the death of his father three years ago 'triggered off my midlife changes.' 'My father, after his retirement, suddenly went downhill and become a total demand on my mother. Although he was the son of a Welsh non-conformist minister, and had always claimed to be a strong believer in nothing after death, actually when it came down to it, he was very frightened of dying.' It made Barry resolve not to make the same 'mistakes' himself, by over-committing himself to work or finding himself reliant on the equivalent of his mother after retirement. As a result he has extricated himself from the working 'treadmill' and steered clear of permanent relationships.
Fathers can give their midlife sons an advanced picture of what they in

turn may end up like thirty years or so further on. At midlife many of the same gestures and mannerisms or ways of handling situations uncannily recall one's own father. Roger Holmbury watches his father now and thinks 'Is this what I will be like in thirty years time? Am I seeing myself as I will then look to others? A daunting prospect.'

Watching his father 'just retire and vegetate' has impelled David Lloyd to be determined to avoid this 'miserable period when you retire'. He's going to make sure he has 'an activity into my seventies' and not become a 'dreary, old depressing bore of a senile man in his seventies or eighties.' He's now full of plans for his post-midlife years as a consequence.

This touches on the notion of the death of the father as a release. Freed from the paternal shadow, a son may now begin to become his own man, fully responsible now for his actions, no longer the 'child' still under a sort of protective umbrella. This freeing process is only properly achieved if accompanied by a mourning and recognition of the dead or dying father. This can sometimes be effected while the parent is still alive. Louis Kaye spent as much time as he could with his father while he was dying in hospital, talking to him about their past together, enabling him to see his father's place in his life and experience the sense of loss while it was happening. An already warm relationship was strengthened and his eventual passing made it easier for both of them, a release shared by both parties.

Paternal shadow can be cast both by a weak father (as in Henry King's case, a 'lovable' but weak man) or by a strong, dictatorial father, as in David Armstrong's case. Both can impel a child to succeed in his own right and establish his own independence.

For David Armstrong this has meant spending much of his life getting away from the dominance of his father. 'I had a very, very severe strict father. I hated my childhood – I absolutely hated it. My father was quite violent in his own way. For a long time I went through life thinking that I was the one that was wrong all the time. I really did.' But it made him determined to make his own way in life, make sure he would not be 'dominated' again. He made mistakes (see pages 20–25), but by trial and error came to discover who he was and what sort of life he needed to live. Now at midlife, he could afford to relax a little in his attitude towards his father. When recently his cousin reminded him that his parents were getting old, he agreed to see them again. 'At that time I was feeling a lot more comfortable and confident and things were going a lot better for me anyway, so I started getting a bit more emotional with them and calling my step-mum 'love' and sending drippy Easter and Christmas cards and all that sort of stuff, and they came to London and they really were very sweet. As a matter of fact the only person who put a suggestively semi-nasty comment in was me and I sort of stopped myself as soon as I said it.' He is making his journey back to his father, very much a midlife task, now the period of exploration and self-establishment of early adulthood is over. It's going back to 'the place where you first started and know it for the first time' to echo T S Eliot's lines.

In Anthony Hyde's case a similar circular journey to the point of origin is taking place. His wish to write a book that would be acclaimed in his father's world, but be written on his own initiative, is an example of this.

Henry Bridges was another who felt under strong paternal pressure. His father's attitude was the classic one of fathers who say 'I'm the boss around here and do as I say.' It made him leave his fatherland in Jamaica to come to London. Much of his self-investigation of the last few years has been to do with trying to come to terms with this: 'some deep pieces of work exploring childhood experiences and paternal influence', as he calls it.

Others, such as Victor Trumper, are still caught up in the double-bind of a hostile relationship with father, unable to detach and distance themselves from it and yet not wishing to express this hostility openly for fear now of 'irreparably' damaging the ageing parent.

At midlife some men are haunted by the fear that they will die at the same age as their fathers, especially when the father died relatively young. Julian Miller's father died aged fifty-nine when he was twenty. It's haunted him ever since, giving his life a sense of urgency to achieve goals and ambitions before he succumbs at the same age. His life has an air of impermanence and frenzied activity about it as a result. He freely admits he is obsessed by death and beset by anxiety that he too will die at fifty-nine. He compares it to the Faustian quest for knowledge and experience before time runs out ('Stand still you ever moving spheres of heaven, that time may cease and midnight never come').

Eric Stratton's father died aged fifty when Eric was a mere nine years old. 'When he died the whole roof came in. I have a picture of him as somebody that everybody liked. He was a family doctor, a GP who shared a practice with his brother. He spent far too long in other people's houses chewing the cud and enjoying the social intercourse, and he was much missed. I didn't realize how much until he died and I'd be confronted by people on the street, who used to grab me by the hand and say "Your dad was such a lovely man". They'd break down on the street in tears which moves me now more than it did then. Then, I was just a bit confused, I couldn't really work it out.' Eric found it difficult to mourn his father's death properly; as a child he was shielded from doing so. But the consequence was that it sent him off into all sorts of different, short-lived directions in his life, from being an HGV driver to a political activist in Nicaragua, haunted by the memory of his father. Now at midlife, still keeping himself young in appearance and in dress, he dreads being the same age as his father was when he died.

Gary Fletcher's case was different. He never knew his father and the details of his death had been kept from him over the years, a family secret.

Then in midlife he set out to find out more. How much had this silence and secrecy been a shadow over his life?

My father died during the war, when I was three, and my mother married again two years later. I've thrown it about in my mind as I'd always wondered what my father would have been like, you know, not having known him. I went through a stage of doing the family tree and that sort of thing, from relatives and from photographs of him and his parents. I was getting quite involved in it and I thought 'Well, I'll get his death certificate'. I knew he'd died the day after my third birthday in Germany and in fact that would have been just after the war ended. My birthday's the middle of June, in '45, and the war ended in May. Then it hit me like a brick; the cause of his death was suicide, he shot himself just after the war, and I didn't know. I had no reason to know up until that point, but my wife knew because my mother had told her. She knew that when I started doing the family tree the chances were that I would find out and it just shattered me. The illusion that I'd had of a father figure for thirty-five years, had been shattered by the fact, I couldn't understand it.

I think somebody could have told me twenty years ago, when I was a man. I think that would have made things easier for me. Yes, it did shatter me a little bit. I think when you dabble with the past, you've got to be prepared for a few shocks. Most families have got them somewhere in the line, but I certainly didn't expect that. It created a problem for me for a while, as I tried to decide whether to find out what the reason was. Had he dipped his fingers in regimental mess problems, or been out with other females? It could have been any number of reasons, or was he just generally ill having been in the artillery in North Africa, Italy and Germany and things had just got too much for him? It was just in peace time, it could have been the guilt that a lot of survivors felt who had lost mates. It could have been any number of reasons and I can appreciate them – people do get very, very depressed and you can be depressed for a matter of seconds and this happens – I will probably will never know the reasons.

He's beginning to come to terms with the shock of this knowledge now and seeing how, at some level, it may have informed his own approach – both as a father himself and in his uncertainties about relationships.

Midlife, then, becomes a time for reflection on both aspects of father-hood: the relationship to father and as a father oneself. Richard West's father wanted him to be a soldier and follow in the family tradition. 'It was tragic for my poor father. He had three sons: the oldest one wanted to be a soldier but failed his exams and never turned into one, while the youngest one is even less a soldier than me. He even sent us to Wellington which is meant to train people into soldiers. I was always quite prepared to be a soldier if I could start off being a General. I couldn't bear the bit in the middle.' Instead he struck out on his own, with considerable success. Now it gives him pause to think on how he has been as a father himself.

I think kids are wonderful. I think it's great having kids around, it is lots of fun having noisy little things challenging for warmth, love and affection for all their impossibilities and difficulties. The way you actually can have a cascade of younger lives in your life is stimulating, enriching and challenges your own life.

Thinking back to his own experience he wonders whether they will in turn follow in his footsteps.

I would be disappointed if they did low-profile, passive things because I suppose one way with your children is to perpetuate yourself. Therefore, if I see things that I recognize in myself in my children, I'm pleased and would like them to go out and compete and win and be victorious. If they chose to do the exact opposite, and there's no reason why they should be the same, I imagine I would feel that they weren't doing all they could with themselves.

Midlife brings the whole question of fatherhood to the fore. The role of father is under scrutiny, and changing. Children are leaving home, calling for less paternal authority, or are going through stages of adolescence that can pose a threat to that paternal authority. Each situation is likely to bring up memories of the father's own adolescence and the way he was fathered himself.

At the other end of the scale come the responsibilities felt towards ageing fathers and parents at this juncture. Often it takes the form of role reversal, parenting the parents. As one interviewee expressed it, the drawback is that '. . . when somebody's dependent on you and goes on treating you as though you're dependent on them, this is really the most awful part of role reversal with your parents – because they do remain your parents. And so there's this sort of blackmailing element of duty allied to this element of authority, which makes it even worse.'

11

Body Change and Death

In the long run we're all dead.

JOHN MAYNARD KEYNES

A constant theme of this book has been that the consciousness of one's own death begins to make itself felt in the early forties. We have seen how this awareness is often brought sharply into focus by the death of parents. Look at the number of interviewees in this book who have described in some detail the impact of the death of their father and found it to be a significant turning point. As the imminence of death makes itself felt, so too do body changes become more noticeable. The all-too-visible signs of age and physical decline begin to show; the back that has held up manfully over the years now begins to give way. How many initial consultations with GPs are over back problems which really mask wider midlife aches and strains? Concern is often expressed over loss of hair, of stamina, of sexual potency, and of erotic appeal, which in turn may account for some of the envy felt towards adolescent children as they begin to experiment with their own sexuality. How often does parental intolerance conceal feelings of competition and secret envy?

The phrase male menopause is often bandied about but it has little basis in fact. Recent research has shown that there is no male equivalent to female menopause. The term most often used is the male climacteric, which the *Penguin Medical Dictionary* defines as 'a nebulous concept for although male fertility gradually declines over the years the change is quantitative rather than qualitative'. Changes in hormonal levels do occur in men after the age of thirty which have an effect on physical status and well-being. A

146

gradual decline in the secretion of testosterone and androgen, the male hormones which affect sexual activity, physical strength and loss of hair and teeth, takes place. There is a diminishing in the size and firmness of the testicles, an enlargement of the prostate gland, a weakening in the force of ejaculation, and a lessening of the amount of the seminal fluid. Erectile responsiveness also slows down, and a shift from the specific genital sensations of youth to more diffuse sensations throughout the body usually takes place – though this in fact can improve the quality of love-making. The male menopause is often used as an 'explanation' for aberrations in male behaviour at midlife. Phrases such as, 'He's going through the menopause' get bandied about but are really indications of the psychological factors we've described earlier, such as the wish to have a last fling, to enact youthful fantasies before the door closes. Symptoms most often associated with the male climacteric are bad temper and an uncharacteristic wilfulness. The French call this phase the *démon du midi*, implying a form of temporary possession, though the word climacteric itself derives from the Greek and means rung on a ladder, which may be a more accurate description.

There is undeniably an increase in psychosomatic conditions at this age. Among our interviewees, we found these variously expressed, sometimes sexually as in the case of temporary impotence or premature ejaculation, or more usually in all sorts of minor ways, such as the person who went for an eye test and carried the prescription round with him for weeks before going to an optician and getting his spectacles.

Stress manifests itself in all sorts of ways. James Henshaw, newly married, worked as a sales rep that took him away from home for many weekends:

. . . a very high profile job with a lot of stress, a lot of pushing other people to do things. Gradually this wore me down until basically my health broke. I went to various doctors and nobody seemed to know what was wrong; had things like tonsils out but they didn't seem to get to the bottom of things. All I wanted to do was out, and my wife backed me fully. She said 'It doesn't matter what we do so long as we are together and we earn enough to live.' At the time I would have swept the streets; I just wanted away from that very high pressure environment. If I'd stayed there would have been a quick coronary on the way, I had reached the pitch where it was either out or under – my body was definitely telling me something.

He did give up his job and moved to the country to find less demanding work running a caravan park.

The cult of fitness, while laudable in itself, is also an attempt to stave off the inevitable ageing process. The body becomes the testing ground in the struggle against time. Feeding the body is a bit like feeding the ego, keeping it topped up, whereas the shadow of middle age brings the need to accept a wider perspective on life, its cyclical nature, the notions of birth, youth and ageing, of eventual decay and death inextricably linked. Fear of change is really a fear of death, of accepting its inevitability.

Joel Aston joined a health club two years back, keen to maintain a high level of fitness and used to go there regularly four times a week. 'Then I dropped it down to only Sunday mornings and now all I do is go to the sauna – I wave at everybody in the gym and go into the sauna, which causes a lot of comment.' He recognizes he's losing the battle to keep fit and healthy and links this to a feeling that 'he might die at any time', a left-over from his sister's sudden and unexpected death when they were both teenagers.

Death stalks the corridors of midlife. Images of old age, infirmity, dependence on others are reinforced by the presence of elderly parents or relatives with distressing signs of physical decline – a reminder and foretaste of how we will be ourselves. Yet death is still something of a taboo subject and we seem to have lost the shared, collective myth about the significance of death and dying; the rituals of mourning are becoming a thing of the past. Each person is left to discover the meaning of death for himself. Technology has played its part in this, diminishing the impact of death so that the sense of awe, finality and the terror are reduced and we are left with what Douglas Dunn terms as 'the antiseptic whiff of destiny'.

Yet, as I have argued through this book, an awareness of death and its inevitability is essential for the midlife transition. Many of our interviewees had a sense of the importance of death at this stage in their lives. Thomas Westfield for one:

I have the gift of faith which makes an enormous difference. I mean I actually look in the 'Deaths' column. Unfortunately, at this age, people one knows are apt to appear in the 'Deaths' columns. The most extraordinary thing is that for all the fun I'm having and it is enormous fun and all the happiness I've got and it is enormous happiness, when I see somebody's death, my first reaction is to think 'lucky him'. But in a sense it's inexplicable because there is nothing but happiness in me and that's absolutely true. I don't know how common that is but it's certainly the case with me.

He is fortunate, perhaps, to have reached this accommodation with death. Earlier he came to realize that it was the fear of the unknown that drove him on and by acknowledging it, harnessing it to his own ends as an entrepreneur, he was able to overcome it, and make use of it. The unknown is like a foreshadow of death ('the undiscovered country from whose bourn no traveller returns'). Thomas Westfield can say he has 'no fear of my own death, I'm impervious to it,' but 'the death of a child, losing the people I love' would be something else. Here he is talking of the sense of continuity provided by children through whom a link to the future and future generations can be made. This is the other accommodation of death, to live on partly through one's children, and partly through one's works. He has family links with India, his grandfather was a missionary there and his father a successful tea broker in Cochin and he himself went there as a young man after leaving university. Recently, linking up again with his past and India, he has adopted a young Indian daughter from Mother Teresa's in Calcutta and she, as he says, 'is enormously important and she has been a symbol of things I don't really understand within myself. I've drawn enormous things from her, drawn a lot from her. Such a courageous child.' Now he plans to commemorate his links with India by building a hospital there in his grandfather's name that will also benefit the less well-off in years to come.

Richard West has also taken stock of his life and acknowledged the increasing importance of an awareness of death at midlife.

Most men see the half-way point in their lives as the equivalent of a menopause. They think they're running out of life and see the gaping grave some distance away and think 'Well, have they been on the planet for a good reason and done all the things that should be done on the planet?' We're only here once. Midlife makes you suddenly, for the first time really, conceive of actually disappearing, dying, going, and wondering whether you've spent your time here very well. And maybe having second thoughts about what you started doing twenty years earlier.

He has set about making sure the second half of his life is filled with meaning for him. For him then, death is acknowledged and incorporated into his scheme of things.

But a more frequently met response is resistance to the idea of death. As Freud wrote 'No one believes in his own death. In the unconscious everyone is convinced of his own immortality.' This wish to preserve immortality ('immortal longings'), to fend off the idea that one is going to die sooner or later, underpins much midlife activity. We see it in the case of an obsessive stepping-up of work, of routines, or a hardening of (moral) attitudes, increased rigidity and an over-controlling approach in relationships, condemning 'others' who may be different, minority groups and so on. It is really a defence against the panic felt at midlife when the onset of physical decline is first experienced as leading to eventual death. Hence the urge to cling tenaciously to the past, to known relationships, and the refusal to let go.

Roger Holmbury would like to end up being an old person who gradually relinquishes his hold on life, able to face death with equanimity. But his dread is of something horrible happening, like a bad illness.

It might be awful, then – like when you imagine yourself in a threatening situation, you think you'll be able to scare your attacker, but when it actually happens, you don't react that way. I've only thought about this in the last year or two, but if I found I'd got bad problems medically, I'd say now I'd certainly want to kill myself. When you're young you think of death as being relatively straightforward and clean. Now that you're older there's always the lingering doubt that you might want to hang on, even under the most hideous circumstances. You might still desperately want to stay alive. There's a Somerset Maugham story of a man who retires to Capri to live comfortably on a ten year annuity, planning to kill himself at the age of sixty-five when it expires. When the time comes, he can't bring himself to do it and is seen wandering round the island, penniless and miserable, a spectre of his former self.

The fear of change and fear of the unknown lead to speculations about after life. Richard West again:

I wish, I wish I was able to believe in the whole dimension of religion and life hereafter. When I get close to snuffing, I might persuade myself that there is one. If I thought I was coming back another time and that I'd come back in some form, depending on what it is, maybe I'd operate differently but I believe I've just got one shot. I think those that can believe in after life are very lucky. It adds that extra dimension to their lives. I just found that my terrestrial logical mind can't make that leap – I'm unable to do that and that I regret. I would love to believe it. I read about a certain number of bright and intelligent people who have converted to Catholicism and I think that's an interesting thing but I can't see myself being able to make that leap, so I think I've only got one time round this track.

Henry King has wondered about this as well.

Occasionally I wake in the middle of the night with a sort of fear 'What the hell is it all about: is it some kind of elaborate joke or why do we have these brains? Is there any sort of other living thing like us in the Universe? What is the Universe? What is the Universe inside? What is it?' I mean, it's an astonishing fact. One simply can't comprehend it can one? But I don't think it makes you believe in Christ. It just makes me in tremendous awe and some fear accepting it, because there's no alternative but to accept it and be determined to try and live positively, because that's all you can do.

It has led him to speculate about life after death.

So one wonders a bit about what's going to happen when you die and I just think it's the end. It's an appalling thought in a way. But I think as one gets older, you get used to it and may even welcome it, because bodily functions change, and you adjust psychologically and physically to dying. Then when it comes, it won't be as appalling as it seems today. Seeing members of my family, uncles and aunts, dying puts me very much more in the lifetime perspective. Being in the middle years makes you treasure it all the more because you realize that time is running out. Seeing the development of infirmity and ill-health in one's friends and relatives and elderly people makes you far more tolerant and determined to make the most of life.'

Barry Hanson defined his midlife changes as moving towards a 'being' model, a flow-with-it approach that puts him in closer touch with the universe. 'Being is making yourself an integral part of nature to the point that it actually doesn't matter whether you're alive or not, it sounds a bit quasi-Buddhist but it does mean that death is such an integral part of life that life after death is not an issue. It's just a different state of being.' He feels that other countries in Asia and Africa understand this much better than we do. 'Why don't we go back to Asia and Africa and recognize that we have an enormous amount to learn from these societies instead of thinking that all we have got to do is export technology round the world?'

Charles Blyth, at the age of thirty, thought he was 'immortal'. Now ten or more years later, he takes a more realistic view.

I'm not looking forward to being elderly. Until I was thirty I just felt almost as if I was immortal. For years and years, I still felt as though I was seventeen or eighteen again. In the last few years I've become more aware of mortality and begin to look and see old people more – you notice the ageing process more and that worries me slightly. I hate the idea of losing my independence and I hope that I stay very, very alert and healthy until the day I die. I would rather die at seventy than go on until the nineties and I would hope that one could have the choice when you are eighty just to die. Certainly I don't want to be senile and I can't imagine if my wife and I are still together in another twenty-five years, which I would hope we are, what would happen if she died first. I can't see that I would really want to go on living for much longer on my own. It's taken nearly twenty years of marriage to find a really very, very good relationship together. That's all got better and better. A lot of dreams we have for the future are very much for us both together. I think I've been very fortunate so I would hate the idea of growing old and depending upon other people for basic needs. I would certainly hate to be alone without my wife and therefore I am much more involved in living life for the present and also building up resources.

Yeats wrote, 'You only begin to live when you have conceived life as a tragedy', in other words, that you will certainly die. Acceptance of this notion can free the individual and give him a clearer path ahead. The alternative can be the chaos and inner turmoil many people experience at midlife, a breakdown, as if trapped in Dante's dark wood, 'savage and harsh and dense'. Acceptance of the finality and inevitability of death gives a sense of release.

12

Summing Up

The unexamined life is not worth living.

PLATO

*Know thyself, know the laws of your own being. Accept them,
even if they seem paradoxical and incompatible with the views
you have grown up with. Live them instead of living the lives
of your parents and grandparents, your neighbours and
professional associates.*

JUNG

In this book I have sought to show the many-faceted nature of midlife. I
hope that these stories, descriptive of personal experience, will serve as
'provocations to thought' and readers will extract what is relevant to them.
The second half of life offers the chance to lead a fuller, more creative life.
It's important to stress that such creativity can be found and expressed in
whatever department of life the individual finds most suitable and appli-
cable to his particular set of circumstances. There is no one path to be
followed nor fixed set of solutions, nor is there necessarily a uniformity to
the passage through midlife. Some people seem to have a midlife crisis
earlier on in their lives, some don't have one at all. Some are born old and
never have a youthfulness to their lives, while others are born young and
strenuously set about manipulating their lives to avoid being old – the Peter
Pan syndrome.

Those that see it as a challenge, a time for stock-taking, for re-appraisal
are usually the ones who fare best. As we have seen, even a full-scale midlife
crisis can brings its benefits. This book has predominantly focused on
situations where midlife was becoming problematic. That way, by going
where the conflicts are, underlying issues can be more easily highlighted.
This is not to ignore the many people who pass through midlife relatively

untroubled. Possibly some of their unease and disquiet goes unnoticed. The burden of this book is that midlife is a crucial watershed and repays being paid full attention to.

Indeed such an emphasis on midlife may be timely. Men's self-awareness and self-understanding are on the increase as men begin to look beyond their traditional narrow bands of responses in times of difficulty. In the past they have usually had recourse to the comfort of stereotypes to measure themselves against – the hero, the doer, the rescuer, the victim and so on. Now a new one can be added – the communicator. Undeniably there's a wish to investigate feelings more openly. It was noticeable how often during these interviews men commented, sometimes with surprise, on how openly and freely they had discovered themselves talking – a pointer surely to an unexpressed, future need to communicate more. The current generation of midlife men, confused about their role and sense of direction, have much to unburden themselves about.

Midlife issues (living in uncertainties, awareness of death, reconciling opposites) replicate key issues of the age we live in. Is uncertainty feasible in international power politics or do we still need to perpetuate the notion of an enemy, itself symbolic of the repressed, unacceptable 'other' half of our natures? The safety net of a deterrent bomb hidden away in a secret arsenal is a metaphor for this one-sided existence, the shadow side of ourselves. It represents a splitting-off, a denial of this other half. Midlife is essentially a mediator between the old and the new and seeks to integrate the split in ourselves and reconcile opposites. For a literary comparison, it is like Prospero casting away his magic wand, able to face the future without its power, 'Now my charms are all o'erthrown and what strength I have's mine own.'

Midlife is a cross-roads. Down one road lies a continuation of the same, the desire to lead a seamless existence. Down the other, a harder path (through Dante's dark wood), lies the struggle to come to terms with midlife issues, face uncomfortable feelings of despair, distrust, anger and frustration, kept at bay over the years but now demanding to be recognized. History cannot be undone, but by accepting the past, the mistakes made, hopes dashed, and then letting go of it, a new dispensation can be found and the future faced with confidence. Many people, as John Cleese has commented, try to get to the grave without ever making a mistake, living out a fantasy that they are different from the way they really are. Midlife, above all, is a time to accept the way 'you really are'.

As we move towards the end of the 1980s and the final decade of the century a *fin-de-siècle* feeling is beginning to show itself. There's a move away from some of the values that have dominated the post-war era (the pursuit of success and status and belief in a world of expanding horizons and material progress) to a concern with more inner-directed living, with the quality of life rather than simply raising the standard of living. As awareness of the limited space and resources of the planet begins to make itself felt, there's a move away from the notion of the quick-fix solution, the short term panacea towards a longer, steadier view of life, an appreciation of the life cycle, of the resources we all contain within ourselves, and which we need to husband, along with those of the planet.

Men, too, are becoming aware of their diminishing resources, their expendability at work where many of their traditional functions are being replicated by technology, or at home where their pre-eminence as head of household is being brought into question. Perhaps this calls for a shift from the traditional male stance to a looser, more uncertain, experimental, playful, help-seeking speculative approach. Such a 'midlife cast of mind' links up with the notion of a journey still going on, as new resources are found through what Jung calls the 'circumambulation of the self'.

Appendix

Hints on how to negotiate the midlife path:

1   Shed the attitudes of a young man.

2   Don't deny parts of your nature. Give them attention. Cultivate ideas, if it suits you. You've only one life and it's yours to live.

3   Lie on your bed, in introspection for days. You won't die.

4   Paralysis, indecision, desire for change, lack of direction, boredom – all are part of midlife. a) So what? b) Accept them c) They'll work themselves out. Nature is self-regulating. Your psyche will work it out and find a solution.

5   Part with anything you used to think important and isn't any longer. Part with it, without regret. Get on with some new things. Sort out what's important now.

6   Life begins at forty, i.e. only by then does one have enough self-knowledge.

7   Have the courage to discard people, entanglements, obligations that are irksome. You've done your bit. Someone else will pick up the burden.

8   Ambition is a curse. Achievement comes from the love of what you do, genuine devotion.

9   Sense of humour. Dust it off.

10   People love us for our faults and candour. So should we.

11   You've nothing to lose, ever.

12   Character is important now rather than being attractive, lively, sexy.

13   Renew old friendships, deepen those with people of the same age.

Adapted from Derek Bowskill, *The Male Menopause*,
[Frederick Muller 1976]

List of Agencies

The following agencies can offer professional help and advice:

MARRIAGE
Relate (formerly National Marriage Guidance Council).
HQ is at Herbert Gray College
Little Church Street
Rugby
Warwickshire CV21 3AP
Tel: 0788 73241.

For nationwide branches see local phonebook under Marriage Guidance –
160 centres.

PSYCHOTHERAPY
British Association of Psychotherapists
121 Hendon Lane
London N3 3PR
Tel: 01 346 1747.

Tavistock Clinic
Adult Department
120 Belsize Lane
London NW3 5BA
Tel: 01 435 7111.

For NHS psychotherapy ask your GP, or call the Department of Psychology in the nearest General Hospital.

COUNSELLING
British Association for Counselling
37a Sheep Street
Rugby
Warwickshire CV21 3BX
Tel: 0788 78328.

GENERAL INFORMATION
Mind, National Association for Mental Health
22 Harley Street
London W1N 2ED
Tel: 01 637 0741.

Institute for Complementary Medicine
21 Portland Place
London W1N 3AP
Tel: 01 636 9543.

Select Bibliography

BELLOW, Saul – *A Theft* (London: Penguin, 1989)

BOWSKILL, Derek and Anthea Linacre – *The Male Menopause* (London: Frederick Muller, 1976)

CONNOLLY, Cyril (Palinurus) – *The Unquiet Grave* (London: Horizon, 1944)

DANTE ALIGHIERI – *The Divine Comedy* (1300)

ERIKSON, Erik – *Childhood and Society* (New York: Norton, 1963)
– *The Life Cycle Completed* (New York: Norton, 1985)

FITZGERALD, Scott – *The Crack-Up* (New York: New Directions, 1945)

FREUD, Sigmund – *Thoughts for the times on war and death* in volume XIV
– *Creative Writers and Day-Dreaming* in volume IX of standard edition of *Collected Works* (London: Hogarth Press and the Institute of Psycho-Analysis, 1959)

GOLAN, Naomi – *Passing through Transition* (New York: Free Press, 1981)

GREENE, Graham – *Ways of Escape* (London: Bodley Head, 1980)

HODSON, Phillip – *Men* (London: BBC Publications, 1984)

JAQUES, Elliot – *Death and the Mid-Life Crisis* in *Work, Creativity and Social Justice* (London: Heinemann, 1970)

JUNG, Carl – *Stages of Life* in *Modern Man in Search of a Soul* (1933) and in *Collected Works*, volume 8 (London: Routledge and Kegan Paul)
– *Selected Writings* edited by Anthony Storr (London: Fontana, 1983)

LASCH, Christopher – *The Culture of Narcissism* (New York: Norton, 1979)

LEVINSON, Daniel J – *The Seasons of a Man's Life* (New York: Ballantine Books, 1978)

MAYER, Nancy – *The Male Mid-Life Crisis* (New York: Doubleday, 1978)

NEUGARTEN, Bernice – *Middle Age and Aging* (University of Chicago Press, 1968)

NORMAN, William and SCARAMELLA, Thomas (eds.) – *Midlife: Developmental and Clinical Issues* (New York: Brunner/Mazel, 1980)

RUSSELL, Bertrand – *How I write* in *Portraits from Memory and Other Essays* (London: Allen and Unwin, 1965)

SAMUELS, Andrew (ed.) – *The Father* (London: Free Association Books, 1985)

SHEEHY, Gail – *Passages: Predictable Crises of Adult Life* (New York: Dutton, 1976)
–*Pathfinders* (London: Sidgwick and Jackson, 1982)

SOLOMON, Kenneth and LEVY, Norman – *Men in Transition* (New York: Plenum Press, 1982)

STEIN, Murray – *In Midlife* (Dallas: Spring Publications, 1983)

STORR, Anthony – *The Dynamics of Creation* (London: Secker and Warburg, 1972)

TERKEL, Studs – *Working* (New York: Pantheon, 1972)

Index